the
book
is
dead

Sherman Young is a senior lecturer in the Media Department at Macquarie University in Sydney, where he convenes the Multimedia degree program. His research focuses on media technologies and their impact on social, cultural and political life. Before becoming an academic, Sherman was a new media designer and producer, and created award winning multimedia products for corporate clients and book publishers.

www.thebookisdead.com

the book is dead.long
live
the
book

SHERMAN YOUNG

NEW
SOUTH

A New South book

Published by
University of New South Wales Press Ltd
University of New South Wales
Sydney NSW 2052
AUSTRALIA
www.unswpress.com.au

© Sherman Young 2007
First published 2007

National Library of Australia
Cataloguing-in-Publication entry

Young, Sherman.
The book is dead (long live the book)

Bibliography.
Includes index.
ISBN 978 086840 804 0 (hbbk.).

1. Books. 2. Books - Forecasting. 3. Book industries and trade. 4. Publishers and publishing.

002

Design Joshua Leui'i
Cover design Di Quick
Printer Everbest

This book is printed on paper using fibre supplied from sustainably managed forests.

⏭ Contents

▶▶| Acknowledgments

Books don't emerge in a vacuum and I must thank my colleagues for the numerous discussions leading to this publication, especially Graham Meikle, Noel King and Angus Phillips who kept the conversation going. The Media Department at Macquarie University provided terrific support, particularly John Potts and Christine Jones. This book only saw the light of day because of the advice and support of my publisher, Pip McGuinness at UNSW Press, and the editing skills of Jessica Perini. Finally, thanks to my family, without whom this book would never had happened; to my mum, dad and sister for filling my formative years with books. And to Amanda, Harper and Truman for reminding me of what is really important.

▶▶I Prologue

She picked up the book and handed it to me. A once pristine copy of Einstein's Dreams *was now a sodden mass of paper-pulp. I tried separating its pages, but they'd turned into the results of a high school chemistry experiment; the green mould growing inside the spine could well have been a new radioactive isotope.*
'You could try the hairdryer; see if that works,' she suggested.
'No,' I replied, a little sadly. 'It's dead.'

We started the renovations a year ago, and began by lovingly packing our books into 68 cartons which we placed in the storeroom in the basement of the house. 'They'll be right,' said the builder. But one missing downpipe and a rare Sydney downpour was all it took for those 68 cartons to be sitting in two inches of water. For what seemed an eternity, the boxes were stuck in the middle of the building site, rotting from the ground up.

Finally, the scaffolding was removed, allowing us to get to the storeroom. Most of the boxes were fine, but the ones on the bottom had sacrificed themselves for the greater good. The cardboard was soaked through; this didn't augur well for their contents. We moved the boxes to the sunshine, opened them one by one, and took out the books. The rot was indiscriminate. *The Man Who Ate Everything* was destroyed alongside *Possession*. *The Beach* survived, but *The Bourne Identity* did not. We wiped every book down and decided which could be salvaged and which could not, unceremoniously tossing each unusable book into the skip, not bothering to make a list because they wouldn't be replaced. Whilst we'd happily pay good money to read a book, we hesitated to pay the same money to keep it, once read.

Between the first sight of the flooded basement, and actually opening the boxes in question, we had come to terms with the fact that all our books may have been destroyed. We were sanguine about that possibility; and over time had realised that the loss of our books was not a calamity. In many ways, those books were already long gone; banished to boxes in a storeroom, inaccessible and unmissed. After all, if you can't find a book (or get to it), it ceases to exist. So cleaning up the wet books was not as painful as I expected. Quite a few perished, but the overwhelming emotion was not one of loss, but of liberation; a realisation that should we move house again, there were a few hundred books we wouldn't have to pack anymore.

The flood may have been divine retribution for daring to write this book; for the audacity to suggest that the book is dead. But it also confirmed the fact that print on paper has its disadvantages. Not only are printed books relatively fragile, they are bulky and heavy; they have to be moved, packed, stored and kept dry. Which is a problem for publishers as well as for home renovators. The entire book publishing industry is constrained by the need to make, move and protect heavy objects. Just as we chose not to replace the damaged parts of our flooded library, publishers must surely baulk at the cost of continuing to print (or even publish in the first instance) books that offer a marginal return on investment. What might change if books had no mass; took up no space? How might publishing decisions be altered? What isn't being published because it's too expensive to turn into a printed object? Just as I had been liberated by the destruction of the object, how might book publishing be freed by that same destruction?

▶▶|

I bought *Einstein's Dreams* on a trip to the Pacific Northwest many years ago. At that time of my life, it was the perfect book. On the outside, a beautiful, small, cloth hardback with a classy paper sleeve. On the inside, a weaving of the literary and scientific worlds in a way which resonated with my own ideas and contradictions. I bought the very first issue of *Wired* magazine on that same trip, and on the flight back to Sydney, *Einstein's Dreams* shared time and space with *Wired* 1.01; the former gesturing to the past just as the latter pointed to the future. The hardcopy of the magazine is long gone, lent to somebody somewhere, or lost in a house move, or dumped in a recycling bin the way magazines are. But I knew that the complete magazine was on the world wide web. I found Issue 1.01, clicked on the first article that caught my eye and read:

> Books once hoarded in subterranean stacks will be scanned into computers and made available to anyone, anywhere, almost instantly, over high-speed networks.[1]

Inspired, and seeking its reincarnation, I googled *Einstein's Dreams*. I searched high and low, but couldn't find an electronic version anywhere; even the dark recesses of bittorrent failed to turn up a pirate version. Only at amazon.com could I find a snippet of the text. I 'looked inside' and read:

> In this world, time is like a flow of water, occasionally displaced by a bit of debris, a passing breeze. Now and then some cosmic disturbance will cause a rivulet of time to turn away from the mainstream, to make connection backstream.[2]

This book is that bit of debris. It argues that what's important about books has long gone, lost in a world whose priorities are shaped by the need to make and move objects. Books die in many ways. They fail to sell and are pulped or left to languish unloved in remainder bins. Or they are not published in the first place, because it is thought that the remainder bin is their most likely fate. Or they are soaked in flooded basement storerooms. Each of these deaths is a consequence of their physical form. For books to live again, a cosmic disturbance is required; separate the book from its object and the book can take on a new life.

The book is dead. Long live the book.

▶▶ CHAPTER 1.
The book is dead

Le Roi est mort. Vive le Roi!

It seems that the book is always about to die. In the last hundred years, the movies, radio, television and the internet have all been drafted as the book's willing executioner. Every few months something emerges to challenge its very existence. In response to the threat, some learned literary figure will pen a thousand word op-ed piece for a newspaper of record in the book's defence and categorically deny rumors of its impending death. Google's stated aim to digitise the known universe has triggered the most recent notices for the imminent demise of the book. In this case, *Wired* magazine's Kevin Kelly fired the first shots[1] and John Updike returned fire in a passionate exchange.[2] This time, both sides are too late. The fact is that the book is already dead.

It doesn't take a genius to see that books no longer sit at the centre of our culture. Our everyday thinking is largely shaped by other media products ranging from television, film, magazines, newspapers, music and the newest electronic bogeymen: videogames and the internet. The book has become a peripheral, a literary fashion accessory for the few who join book clubs or go to writers' festivals. Both anecdotally and statistically, no-one reads books anymore. Look around next time you're on a bus or train and count how many books are being read. Compare that number with the tally of (mostly white) headphones dangling out of ears. Or if you're in a large city, indulge in a little real estate porn and visit a few open houses. Whilst you're sticky-beaking, count the books, and make a note of whether they're lying open on coffee tables, or sitting dog-eared on shelves. Both exercises confirm what the surveys tell us: people aren't reading books. Then visit your local bookstore. If you don't have one, you're not alone. Bookselling is being concentrated into the megamall experience. Two years ago, there were two independent bookshops in my local shopping area. Today there are none. And it seems that every time you turn around, another small publisher has gone bankrupt, or been amalgamated into a bigger multinational concern.

But wait, counter the book-lovers. More books are being published than ever before. Whilst smaller bookshops might be closing, you can buy books in more places; supermarkets, chainstores, even on the internet. And those big bookstores are vast, offering more miles of bookshelves than ever before. All of this might be true. But the book is still dead.

Apart from its relegation to the cultural sidelines, it is dead because most books published and sold are more 'anti-book' than book. There may be more titles available in the closest Borders store; there may be books in between the confectionary aisles of every supermarket in the country. But they are books *in name only*. The vast majority of books do not speak to the 500-year history of book publishing; they are not part of what might be called *book culture*; a culture centred on *ideas* and furthering the human conversation.

We still have objects called books. We still have businesses that publish and sell those objects. But the unique value that books contribute to our essential humanity has been increasingly diluted. Despite its age and traditions, book publishing is not mass media; nothing is more niche than solitary authors expounding on the topic of their own pet cactuses. And in the last 30 years or so of trying to become a hit-driven mass-media form, the book industry has killed the book. Take a stroll around your local megastore. Avoid the coffee shop and the DVD section. Move past the mp3 players and reading lights. Take away the ghostwritten sports autobiographies, ignore the celebrity cookbooks and cynical movie tie-ins. Bin the self-help books (*Everything you need to know about books you learnt when your house burnt down whilst you were changing the colo(u)r of your parachute*) and the cash register stocking fillers. What's left? Not a lot.

Some time in the last half of the twentieth century the business of books changed. The intellectual butterflies of the publishing industry devolved, not into caterpillars but slugs, as they were absorbed borg-like by multinational corporations intent on taking an industry that traded on *ideas*, into one which traded in those ideas on some fast-buck shifting of product. Books became yet another victim of the apparent need to redefine return on investment in terms of purely short-term monetary gain. For whatever reason, we have decided that books (like universities) now have to pay their own way and do so in a very short period of time. The idea of public good has been largely cast aside as the zaniness of soft-headed hippies from a bygone era.

Consider this. The process of producing books demands a real investment of resources. Making books is expensive. As is selling them. By contrast, writing books is comparatively cheap, demanding few resources beyond the time of a committed author, many of whom write for reasons other than money. This tension has a couple of consequences. Firstly, the book trade has always sat on the cusp of culture and commerce, as what Laura Miller calls 'reluctant capitalists';[3] it has traditionally been peopled by a balance of those who were conscious of their role in the remaking of cultures and others who understood that books were a *business* and that success was about getting the culture/commerce balance correct.

Secondly, books have long been shaped by time, and getting the aforementioned balance correct has largely been about taking time to do things the right way. It used to be understood that books were a craft, and required sustained effort. It was expected that authors had to be supported and nurtured and worthwhile ideas sometimes took years to emerge; ideas which, once formed, had to stand the test of hindsight. Moreover, the culture was one where literary genius was measured in longevity; where a publisher's backlist – books that often were written decades ago – was their most valuable asset, and a canonical list of classics existed based on that longevity.

But the book's relationship to time has altered dramatically in the last few decades. As befits the modern publisher's reinvention as a small part of one of a few global multimedia enterprises, time is no longer privileged. Publishers are under increasing pressure to turn out new titles. New authors are given very little opportunity to sell and warehouses do not hold extensive backlists. Part of the change is a reflection of modern social and economic activity; speed is the new mantra, and the book trade is not immune to the pressures of quarterly financial reporting and weekly sales figures.

▶▶ New technology and all that

Most discussions about the death of the book suggest that new technologies will deliver the requisite death blow. The age of print, said Marshall McLuhan,[4] will give way to an electronic one. And tech-pundit after tech-pundit has promised that radio, television, CD-ROMs or the internet will kill the book. They were all right, but in an unexpected way.

Electronic media did not slay the book by replacing it. Whilst there has been displacement, and the tome is now just one of many media options, something more subtle and complicated happened. In trying to preserve the printed form of the book, the book trade was happy to change its contents to suit the shifting publishing environment. In order to save the object, the book was changed into something else entirely. Electronic media killed the book by forcing book publishers to adapt to the faster pace of information flows; to evolve into something more appropriate for the E! generation. Printed books have become more like television shows; the need for speed and instant gratification has resulted in the anti-book object that dominates today's book trade. Books are now designed to capitalise on particular moments; to leverage off other media assets; to profit from corporate synergies; to buy into the five minutes of fame demanded of modern celebrity culture; and to pander to the get-rich-quick schemes that pass for self-help. And books themselves reflect this cultural shift, with shorter chapters, fewer words, splashier graphics and absolutely no ideas. What's more, these books are now given only a few months to be successful before they are yanked off the shelves.

You could probably mark the beginning of the end with the invention of the telegraph; the moment when information began to move more quickly than goods. Since then, the book has found breathing more difficult. Follow its long slow demise through to the concentration of global multimedia empires in the late twentieth century, where it struggles on, choking for air.[5] But to suggest that the book has run out of oxygen solely because of technological change is too determinist.

In fact, *new technologies will save book culture*. Computer-based communications, social networks and newly de-institutionalised creativity can play a role in re-privileging the *idea* of ideas. The essence of the book can be captured and distilled from its material form; the new technologies can form the basis for a reinvigoration and a reinvention of book culture. Rather than cling desperately to the old ways, we should embrace the opportunities presented by the new.

The *object* of the book is the problem. Whilst it's easy to blame Nielsen Bookscan,[6] part of the change can be attributed to the limitations of the physical form of the book. The act of printing, binding, shipping and storing paper bundles around the planet is anachronistic. The time and resources that could be spent ensuring that a book culture continues is wasted on creating objects; cultivating trees instead of ideas. The constraints caused by having to *print books* impedes the potential inherent in writing and publishing them. Modern publishing is not about shifting ideas, it's about shifting objects.

And it often appears that the content is relevant only insofar as making the object appealing enough to sell. Publishers' concerns centre around the cover and the blurb; about making the object (or container) sufficiently appealing that someone will pick it up and buy it. Tom Dyckhoff, writing in the *Guardian*, sums up the game at hand:

> Publishers have just a few seconds to catch your eye, as you promiscuously scan the shop floor. Let your eye rest for a second, and they've almost got you. Make contact, read the blurb on the back and, most importantly today, clock the face of the author.[7]

The book is dead because the book trade is about selling objects, not ideas.

▶▶ Books don't matter

Of course, a *book* called 'The Book is Dead' is an absurd proposition. The very fact that you are holding it in your hands suggests that its central premise is flawed. Or that it's an example of the worst excesses of the age: a cheap (so-called) post-ironic statement designed by the marketing department of a struggling book publishing company. Which is, of course, what it is. Apart from the bit about my publisher being a struggling company. And maybe this book is postmodern, not in any cynical marketing way, but because it is 'a map preceding the territory', and its self-referential character must be excused because its fate as a book might demonstrate the truth of its title. That the book is dead.

Think about this. This book was commissioned in late 2005 and written during the course of 2006. Although it wasn't the only thing I did that year, the book did take up an awful lot of my 'brain space', and whether I was jotting down ideas, reflecting on some observations, chatting to like-minded people or actually typing words on my computer, it was my major project of 2006. When I first talked to my publisher, we threw around some potential sales figures. With any luck, she said, it will sell 3000 copies. That's it. It'll make my publisher a little money and somewhat less for me. Maybe enough for a new stove, we joked. But like most authors, money wasn't the motivating factor. Being an academic, I'm more interested in ideas. And if my luck holds, the concepts contained in these pages will be read by a few thousand people; one or two of whom might actually engage further in a conversation about the future of books.

Of course this is more people than read my doctoral thesis (a grand total of four) or most journal articles, but it's still not a lot. Even in academia. To put it into some perspective, I regularly lecture to classes of several hundred undergraduates. Granted, most of them probably pay no heed to what I'm saying, but who knows what proportion of my buyers will be readers, or will read this book *all the way through*. No matter how hard you spin it, this book is a mere blip, a few thousand readers is miniscule. And it's probably no different from many others that have been published. Some American statistics: in 2004, only 10 book titles sold more than a million copies. Fewer than 1500 sold more than 50 000 copies. Sixty-seven thousand titles sold between 1000 to 5000 and most books published sold fewer than 99 copies.[8] Most books have almost zero cultural impact. They simply don't matter to most people.

Of course, *some* books do have a much larger impact. The most popular books manage to shape contemporary culture for a few minutes. Some are even made into Hollywood blockbusters. And a handful become book to film to videogame multimedia empires. The majority of those are seldom what the Saturday supplements call literary. And the idea that an 'intellectual' book will be a mega-seller is normally just silly. There are exceptions that prove the rule; some bestsellers are not airport-bookshop-blockbusters. For example, over nine million copies of Stephen Hawking's *A Brief History of Time* are in print.[9] Even I have a copy on my bookshelves where it sits ready to impress visitors. But I have no idea what it's about because I haven't read it. In fact, I've only met one person who has read *any* Hawking book from cover to cover, and he works for NASA. A lot of people know of Stephen Hawking from his appearance on *The Simpsons* rather than from anything he's written. Maybe a book's impact on the wider cultural fabric is some kind of trickle-down effect; a series of 'Chinese whispers' emanating from the few who have read the book to the many who like to say they have. Those who don't bother with the book and just read the reviews. Tom Townsend, a character in Whit Stillman's 1990 film *Metropolitan* sums it up:

> I don't read novels. I prefer good literary criticism. That way you get both the novelists' ideas as well as the critics' thinking.[10]

▶▶ㅣ Does anybody still read books?

Most people don't read books. A much-cited US National Endowment for the Arts survey[11] from a couple of years ago confirms that there is a downward trend in reading books of any kind. For too many people, reading books is associated with school, or work of some kind; it is a chore rather than a pleasure. It probably begins differently. Middle class kids are encouraged by schemes such as the Premier's Reading Challenge and Children's Book Week. All the 'how-to-bring-up-kids' gurus declare that parents should read three books to their kids every night before bedtime. But reading appears to become less important as children get older. My extended family is a statistically insignificant case in point. My kids are four and five and love their books. The brightly coloured pictures and simple rhymes of childhood favourites make bedtime a treat for the four year old, and the older child is busy trying to sound out new words as she works through her home readers. On the other hand, I have several nephews. The seven year old still reads; mainly *Scooby Doo* stories, but more recently football magazines. He spends more time watching cartoons. His cousins are 10 and 13. The 10 year old plays Xbox incessantly and never goes anywhere without his Game Boy. His brother has a *World of Warcraft* account and dips into the virtual at every opportunity.

Interestingly, all of these children are surrounded by books. We regularly give books as birthday and Christmas presents, and the entire adult family is one of book readers. Of course, kids seem to obsess fanatically for short periods of their lives. It wouldn't surprise us if one of the boys devoured the *Lemony Snicket* series over one summer holiday. But even if he does, books aren't the focus of childhood leisure time. On top of the childhood activities of my day, a plethora of media and play opportunities now exist. I may have mucked about with bicycles and watched television when I was young, but I didn't surf the web when I was five. Both my kids already do; clicking links with a mouse as naturally as they turn the pages of a book. As children get older, the distractions become even more plentiful and squeezing books into the demands of adult life is not a choice that many seem to make.

The industry responds with the claim that book sales are still healthy; that more book titles are being published than ever before. And that blockbusters keep selling in the millions. If the book is dead, they argue, what about Dan Brown and JK Rowling? But take away the superstar authors and the numbers trail to literally nothing. In Australia, the tenth biggest selling paperback of 2005 sold 'over 55 000 copies'.[12] Which seems like quite a few until you realise that the same number of people will sit in the rain at the Melbourne Cricket Ground watching *one* football game. And they'll do it every Saturday in winter.[13] Or that in order to make the top 10 television shows on any given night, over a *million* people need to be watching.[14] And in case you're wondering, the Australian data is pretty similar to the overseas experience. In 2002, Alice Sebold's novel *The Lovely Bones* was a mega-hit, selling 1.5 million copies. That same year, Fox debuted the television series *Skin* which attracted four times that number of viewers, but was considered a dismal failure and cancelled.[15] Without entering into the debate about the accuracy of television ratings numbers, it's clear that books and television occupy completely different realities when it comes to audiences.

Patently, reading books is a niche activity, something we'll discuss more in Chapter 3. However the demise of the book should not be confused with the death of reading. Despite declining sales, people *are* still reading newspapers and magazines. Even those pimply teenage boys are reading walk-through guides for their PlayStation games. And the web is (despite temporary video phenomena such as YouTube) a largely text-driven place. So people are reading websites, blogs and chats. Reading (and writing) are still part of everything we do. At which point, booklovers are known to get defensive and start to mutter unkind things about 'the internet'. Books will be around forever, they say. And they roll out the usual arguments about cost, convenience, portability, the ease of reading ink on paper instead of a flickering screen and the evil panopticon that is the world wide web.[16] Despite their protestations, the book is dead. The bottom line is that there are now better ways of reaching an audience than publishing a book in the old-fashioned way. Perhaps we need to think about publishing books in a new-fashioned way.

▶▶ In the beginning

Johannes Gutenberg's use of movable type made mass produced printing feasible and revolutionised book publishing. He was voted Man of the Millenium[17] for this feat, which many claim changed the world. Within 30 years, Europe went from a continent starved of reading material to one 'peppered with around nine million books'.[18] The accepted wisdom is that the book greatly contributed to (amongst other things), the Enlightenment, the Renaissance and the creation of modern science.[19] Pedants (and the more culturally sensitive) might point to the Chinese invention of movable type 300 years earlier,[20] but it's undeniable that western literary tradition and culture owes a more direct debt to Gutenberg than Pi Sheng. Gutenberg worked in Mainz on the Rhine River in Germany, about midway between Frankfurt and Koblenz. I visited nearly two decades ago as part of a gap-year ramble around the planet, and it didn't make much of an impact. All I remember is that it was raining and I sought shelter in the Gutenberg Museum where I spent some time out of the drizzle looking at a copy of his eponymous bible.

What struck me about the *Gutenberg Bible* is how similar and how different it is to a modern book. It's instantly recognisable as a book; printed on paper pages, bound into a single object and read in a way familiar to us all. It was also singularly different from the copy of *Let's Go Europe* that I was lugging around at the time. Look closely at the *Gutenberg Bible*, and the style of the text is reminiscent of a hand-copied manuscript. And whilst the words and lines were printed, each copy was individually coloured by artists, making it unique. In many ways, the *Gutenberg Bible* is like most examples of transient technologies. It is a hybrid; a combination of the old and the new, in which a new technique is used to recreate the look and feel of an older media form. What's more, only 180 copies were printed. At the time, it was an unheard of number, but it's a long way from the massive print runs publishers require today. Consistent with this miniscule print run and in another parallel to today's publishing world, Gutenberg apparently made no money from his bibles.

Books have obviously changed a lot since Gutenberg's time. Printing and binding techniques improved, distribution channels became far more efficient and an entire industry sprung up around the book 'object' of the codex. And the book as object continues to change. The bound codex of the early twenty-first century is not that of a hundred years ago. *The Da Vinci Code Special Illustrated Edition* (paperback), with its combination of text and graphics, interplay between fiction and non-fiction and marketing-driven format would have been unimaginable in an era of fragile cloth-bound hard-cover books. The nineteenth-century reader would be confronted by graphic design, manifest in new typefaces and striking covers matched with totally unheard of visual and textual arrangement. In the last hundred years, we have seen the invention of the paperback, the various trade formats and comic books. Notwithstanding the differences evident in today's books, pick up an old book and place it next to a new one and the disparity is enormous. All of which suggests that the object of the book is not fixed and *has always been evolving.*

The sheer heft of old volumes has given way to paperbacks as people demanded portability, or found other ways of reading that better suit their requirements. Some now find that even the paperback is too physically constraining. On the Lonely Planet discussion forums, responding to 'what one book would you take travelling?', 'pq' suggests: 'Download some talking books onto your iPod and take as much as you want. Books are just too heavy.'[21] For pq, there is no suggestion that an audiobook is anything other than a book. It is merely the most obvious solution to a problem of portability that every traveller has experienced. Some read on their smartphones:

> For me, it's primarily about availability of the device – I hate carrying around stuff. I have a treo 600 that's taken over a great deal of my PC tasks. I never started reading e-books until I got it ... Anyway, I've done so much reading with the treo (wherever I find myself waiting I can read) and gotten used to the convenience of not turning pages, having my place saved automatically in multiple books, having a backlight

so that ambient lighting is irrelevant, having all the books
I've read on the device present for reference and electronic
searches, that I have a hard time picking up a paper book
now.[22]

Both these readers understand that they are still reading books.
But for them, the object has evolved into one that no longer
involves print on paper. Whilst such readers are currently in
the minority, they represent a possible future for the book; one
in which the object is allowed to evolve into something quite
different.

▶▎   What is a book meant to do?

Ask most people to define a book, and they would look at you
as if you were stupid. 'It's obvious,' they would say, speaking
slowly. 'A book is something that you read. It's a collection of
bound paper pages containing useful or entertaining text.' But
the obvious doesn't always reflect the complexity of reality. A
book is *not* just that thing in your hands. If we allow books to be
defined solely by their material form, we miss the point. We need
to think about what books are *meant to do* and be open minded
enough to consider whether the object is still required.

The telephone makes a terrific analogy. Thirty years ago
the telephone in my parent's living room was a large, heavy
beige plastic device with a rotary dial. It was fixed, located in a
specific room in a house. Telephone calls were made from one
location to another and the device was only capable of allowing
a synchronous voice conversation to occur between two people.
Think about what the telephone was *meant to do* 30 years ago.
Most countries recognised the public service value in a national
telephone network and instituted universal service obligations
which required telephone companies to deliver their service
to the entire population at a reasonable cost. The telephone
infrastructure was usually run by a national monopoly, reflecting
the importance of the phone network. Cross-subsidies were

commonplace, and as a result, so-called local calls cost very little, or were free.

Today, what we call a telephone is a tiny pocket-sized device that is linked to a *person* not a *place*. As well as allowing us to speak to each other, phones transmit text, pictures and video messages. More often than not, they also play videos and music, surf the web and annoy those around you with downloadable ringtones. The company behind the phone and its infrastructure are probably stockmarket darlings trying to make big bucks in a competitive marketplace. Think about what a telephone is *meant to do* today, and affordable local calls in the national interest would not be very high on the agenda. Timed local calls, high costs between networks (particularly with mobile telephony) and a switch in priority which has seen telephone companies focus on more profitable services has killed that old fashioned idea of the telephone. In short, there are still devices called telephones and they can still be used for voice conversations over a distance. But the telephone, as we knew it, is dead. Ironically, voice-on-ip services (such as Skype) which build on internet connected personal computers have become the mechanism for that old idea of a telephone to re-emerge, allowing cheap location-to-location calling on devices that currently don't look much like the telephones of yesteryear.

The book is the same. Cultural habits and motivations have changed. The production process is dramatically different, as are the corporations involved and the values embedded in that process. The book you hold in your hand is less likely to speak to ideas of a book culture than a superficially similar one produced 50 years ago. Today, books are vehicles for cross-promotion of high-profile multimedia products. They are branded, manufactured entities whose purpose is to leverage the synergies that exist in global corporations. Think *Harry Potter* and his miscellaneous wizardry paraphernalia. Or any other successful franchise. And ask the question: 'Is *this* what books are meant to do?' Just as voice-on-ip does telephony better than telephones, maybe there are better ways of doing books.

So why bother writing or publishing a book now? Because this is a time of opportunity, as well as crisis. The book as we know it may be dead, but just as a king's demise often leads to a renewed kingdom, acknowledging the book's death is the first step in its rebirth. Then we can remember that it's *what books do* that is important, not *what they are*. Writing a book entitled *The Book is Dead* creates a delicious irony, but hopefully this merely marks the beginning of a longer conversation. One which will take place in any number of public forums. That the book is dead should not be cause for commiseration. Rather, we should celebrate what books *can do* and embrace the emerging opportunities. This printed book may only be read by 1000 people. Its contents might wither and die at the end of a particular branch of publishing history. And in doing so, its central premise will be fulfilled. Or the ideas in this book may resonate and take a life of their own; they may be discussed and debated in a hundred new forums, spreading the conversation about books far and wide. The object that is this book will be forgotten, even as its ideas take a life of their own.

In many ways, this book is a plea for what's *inside* books to become more valued. And if that means that new ways of spreading the word, new engagements with the text are required, then so be it. We need to salvage the book's essential organs by discarding the decaying body. The book's heart will beat more strongly elsewhere. After all, words still matter, they continue to shape who we are as people and define what is important to us. Many people still read and write, pause and reflect, engage with the fabric of human existence via words and images in ways that printed books have done for centuries. Only now, the most vibrant ideas, the most scintillating conversations, the very essence of *book culture* has migrated elsewhere. Away from the traditional publishers and booksellers. And into other hands and other spaces.

The media technologies that have put downloaded talking books on pq's iPod are important for other reasons. They enable entirely new ways of engaging with content. Like it or not, readers are becoming writers. The imagined human conversation that used to take place *between the books* is now something everyone can see. And participate in. As in many other realms, the internet is making the invisible visible. Where once authors were blind to the reaction that a book might provoke (apart from in the minds of a few published critics, and the odd festival crowd), today they can expose their frail egos to a virtual battering and easily continue the conversation that their books begin. Which begs the questions: 'Why not just create a website, or a blog and write in that space? Isn't a blog a more accessible, convenient, and timely replacement for a book on any particular topic? Aren't boingboing.net or fark.com better ways to express the quirky entirety of popular culture than any printed artefact on the same theme?'

Despite the title of this tome, I think not, and we'll examine why in more detail later. Whilst the book as an object is dead, its place in the cultural milieu is essential and must be protected. There are things that books can do, characteristics that they possess, conversations that they allow that must be preserved. In the same breath that I call the book dead, I make a plea to hold onto the essence of *what a book should do*. Having cast aside the notion that the book is an object, the next step is to identify exactly what a book is. Cultural theorists[23] reckon that the hardest part about analysing a cultural object is defining it. And that's what I'll do in the next chapter.

▶▶❙ CHAPTER 2.
What is a book?

What's in a name? that which we call a rose
By any other name would smell as sweet ...

William Shakespeare

Every year, the Children's Book Council of Australia holds Children's Book Week, designed to encourage kids of all ages to read and keep reading. Typically, the week ends in a parade, when school children are encouraged to dress up as their favourite *book* character for the day. They love it because rather than doing sums in class, they get to romp around the school grounds for a few hours and laugh at the funny costumes worn by their teachers. Not to mention the kids. At my daughter's school, the usual suspects from nursery rhymes walked hand in hand with several Cats in the Hat, Wallies (of *Where's Wally* fame) and numerous Aslans and Harry Potters. It was difficult to tell if the latter two were book characters or movie characters though. At least they began life on the page, which is more than can be said of all the parading pirates; I thought that Jack Sparrow was born in a theme park ride. Jack was surrounded by cartoon characters and comic book superheroes, which I suppose came from 'graphic novels'. Also doing laps of honour were several cricketers, an anonymous racing car driver and sundry rugby league and soccer players. All in all, an eclectic mix that probably paid more attention to *Nickelodeon* or *Fox Sports* than HarperCollins.

Some fellow parents tut-tutted at the rather broad interpretation of *books*, and the headmaster seemed to empathise. He introduced the parade and congratulated all the kids for coming as their favourite characters from 'books [pause], television and the movies'. It didn't matter, he said, 'because they all began as books; as words written in a story'. And maybe he's right. At the very least he'd summed up the complexity of the question at hand.

So, what is a book? The obvious answer is that a book is what you're holding in your hands right now; a few hundred pieces of paper, pages covered in printed ink and bound together. A portable object that contains words and pictures which people can look at or perhaps even read. An object that houses stories, thoughts, ideas and which might even provide occasional clues about our world and the absurdity of its humanity. And because that content is so varied – ranging from self-obsessed autobiographies through to cartoon pornography – the *object* takes pride of place. The obvious answer to the question lies in the very materiality of the thing in your hands. But that answer is wrong.

A multitude of comic books, illustrated books and novels, picture books, cook books and encyclopedias, academic monographs, travel guides and compilations of case law topple from library bookshelves. The *White Pages* and a catalogue of hydraulic hose fittings are books, but try reading one of those to your five year old at bedtime. *Pilates for Dummies* has as much in common with the *Complete Works of Shakespeare* as the Sydney Opera House has to a bus shelter. It's not just a matter of genre or categorising. Defining a book by its material form misses the point entirely; something instinctively understood by the headmaster of my daughter's school. So what *is* a book?

▶▶ The book machine

A book is a *technology*. We tend to think of technologies as things to do with computers, and forget that they encompass the complete range of human accomplishments. We forget, for example, that language, reading and writing are technologies. The book, that apparently simple object, manufactured from ink and paper is part of a technology that is so entrenched in our culture that we take it for granted.

What's more, all technologies are *systems*: a combination of an object, the processes that created that object, and *ideas about that object*. So, the *object* of the book is merely one part of a technological system, or *assemblage*, as French theorists might describe it. And that object might be the least important part of the assemblage.

An example. Consider the humble brick. In itself, it's a lump of clay, moulded into a particular shape. It can be used to build a wall or thrown through a plate glass window. It is only when a brick is part of a technology that it is properly defined. Informed by ideas of construction, urban design, quantity surveying, design and aesthetics, *bricklaying*, the humble brick has literally built the world. As part of the technology of vandalism, it does something completely different. It is not the object itself, but the system surrounding it which defines its actual worth. In other words, the most important part of a technology are the *ideas which inform it*; what Gilles Deleuze and Felix Guattari call its *abstract machine*.[1]

Ideas can be technical, social, cultural, economic or overtly political. But think of the motivation behind a technology, and its essence becomes clearer. For example, buses and cars share many things. Both have wheels, an engine of sorts and use our public (and private) road systems. They have similar engineering components in their suspension and drivetrains. And they even share the idea of freedom of movement (unlike trains or trams whose movements are constrained by tracks). Buses might be bigger (in the same way that the *Times Atlas of the World* is bigger than a Jeffrey Archer novel) and to the untrained eye, buses and cars share a physical similarity. But buses and cars are fundamentally dissimilar. The ideas which drove their development are not the same, nor is their usage. The car is derived from a notion of personal freedom, rooted plainly in the private realm. The bus has a communal basis and largely exists as a public good. Not too many individuals drive buses.

And so it is with books. A book is not just 200 paper pages, with ink-printed words and an appealing cover. It is a combination of ideas, cultural practices and industrial processes. Whilst books share an apparently similar material form, the reasons for their existence and the cultures they inhabit may be poles apart. *Green Eggs and Ham* and *Hansard* might be superficially similar, but they exist for completely different reasons and emerged from two completely different contexts. Yet they are both considered books; sharing a basis in print technologies.

At one extreme, it's possible to understand two seemingly identical books as motivated by entirely different ideas. For example, the original Jonathan Cape edition of William Faulkner's novel *As I Lay Dying* exists for very different reasons than the Random House *Oprah Book Club Box Set* released in 2005. The original edition is testimony to an older, somewhat romantic, book culture. Writing of his publishers of the time, Jason Epstein notes that:

> it was well known that for years Bennett and Donald had supplied Faulkner with money, paid his overdue bills … nursed him through his love affairs, his drunken nights, his hangovers … and tried, not always successfully to keep his books in print when few people wanted them. This act of faith cost both time and money.[2]

The Oprah Book Club edition is an example of modern publishing, a repackaging of an existing title so as to extract revenue at minimal cost. The same book; different abstract machines. The energy and expense that might have been devoted to nurturing a modern-day Faulkner instead goes into the marketing and promotion (or cross-promotion) of a special edition of a long-dead author whose legacy and sales would have been adequate in any case; the promotion of an existing canon taking precedence over the search for successors.

But I digress. Those issues will be pondered in more detail later. The point is that the answer to the question 'What is a book?' is a complex one, that comes down to identifying a common abstract machine, a key idea or meme that makes books unique, and that still distinguishes a Patrick White novel from the *NSW Road Rules*. We need to answer the question I flagged in Chapter 1: 'What is a book meant to do?'

▶▶ǀ Print ≠ books

Some suggest that the abstract machine in question is a thing called *print culture*; the history and legacy of mass produced print that has defined much of the civilised world. Many have argued that the key to books is the technology of printing; that the centuries since Gutenberg's printing press have seen the emergence of a culture predicated on that technology. Elizabeth Eisenstein argued that print allowed for radical social change; such as the Reformation and the idea of universal literacy.[3] Walter Ong suggested that print allowed for more subtle cultural change; that the arrangement of print on paper created a communications space that brought about, amongst other things, the idea of finality or closure.[4] Marshall McLuhan also suggested that a literary or print culture emerged as a result of that printing press; effectively displacing the previous oral culture and ensuring the emergence of a way of life in which writing, reading and looking things up became more important than speaking, listening and remembering things.[5] Of course, the lament of some (such as Neal Postman[6] and McLuhan[7] again) is that this print age has itself been displaced by the electronic age; that first radio and television, and now computers and the internet have shifted the emphasis from print to screen.

There is a subtext in that line of thought which equates *print* with *book*, privileging the object with no attempt to understand the complexity of the book as a technological system. Which is wrong.

The technology of the book *can* involve the same technology as *printing*. Printing is a process that puts images on paper using ink. The former might utilise the latter, but its focus is more precise. In defining the book, we should pay less attention to the technology of *printing* and more to the technology of *book publishing*. Printing technologies are not *book* technologies; there is more to a book than just printing something on paper.

There are three distinctive elements which comprise the technology of the book. The first is the book's content, the *ideas* that an author is attempting to communicate. Theorists use the term 'text', and without (yet) entering into debates about the nature of authorship, it is a useful way to consider the idea of a book. Traditionally, print culture has situated such 'texts' as words and pictures on the page, but alternative ways of communicating texts already exist. Audiobooks, for example, attempt to replicate the fidelity of the text, whereas film adaptations or multimedia productions draw on what might be considered its intrinsic elements. All draw from the ideas of the author.

The second component of the book is *publishing*. The publishing industry, because it *creates* books *defines* what a book is. The book has long been defined by its relationship with those who publish, and whose role has been to provide the necessary expertise and infrastructure to allow authors access to editorial, marketing and distribution. A closer analysis of its history and evolution can be found elsewhere, but book publishers play three key roles in defining both the book as text and the book as object. The first is in creating the book (both as text and as object). Whether texts are acquired through acquisition meetings, with titles from new and established authors presented by publishing directors; or whether they are driven by marketing departments who identify a niche and commission a title to fill it; books as texts are nurtured by editors until they are in a form that is acceptable to the publisher. Simultaneously, the book as object is defined. Designers conceive of aesthetic parameters, drafting cover designs and playing with typography and page layout.

The second part of the publisher's role is in marketing (or selling) the book. Overwhelmingly, the role of marketing is intruding on the role of creation,[8] but for the purpose of this analysis, I'll ignore this overlap. Once the book has been created, it has to be sold. In this part of the industry, marketers decide on formats and print runs; and publicity departments create the buzz that contextualises the forthcoming title and distinguishes it from the mass of other 'soon to be' releases. Sales reps pitch books they have never seen to bookstores who try to guess the zeitgeist, protected by generous sale or return policies.[9]

The bookstores represent the final act of the publishing industry: that of distribution. Once a title has passed muster with publishers and editors, and been run through the marketing machine, it enters the channel which begins in distribution warehouses and ends in bookselling superstores in suburban shopping malls.[10] At a mass market level, the would-be bestseller jumps through all these hoops; sometimes aided by massive marketing, PR and advertising campaigns. The process for smaller titles and those from independent presses differs only in scale. The role of the publisher remains the same; create, market and distribute.

The final component that defines the book is the object itself. Whilst the content or text might be repurposed or reconfigured for alternative media forms, the artefact of the printed book has physical characteristics. Each edition of a book has a heft, texture, touch and even smell that has cultural value in itself. Type printed on paper, bound into a manageable and affordable object allows easy legibility, portability and collectivity. There is also an aesthetic appeal that embraces ideas of typography, graphic design and the visceral reaction gleaned from a particularly attractive first edition hard cover. Those who 'love books' are often attracted to the object as much as the ideas; their library's shelves overflowing with titles that provide them with touchstones of identity, and a particular status. As author Nick Hornby suggests 'all the books we own, both read and unread, are the fullest expression of self we have at our disposal'.[11] Five minutes spent examining bookshelves on a first date makes it much easier to decide whether to have a second one.

Some appreciate the ability to bookmark, notate, dog-ear corners and interact with the object of the book in a tactile manner. As much as the text of a book is key, for many, the book as an object is similarly essential. But the object, *by itself*, is not the book. It is only in combination with the other two components – the text, and publishing – that a book comes into being. And there is no reason why the object need remain, forever, in the form with which we have become so familiar. Already some people are comfortable with reading on screens, or listening to audiobooks. Whilst the printed object has served the book well for a long period of time, it has limitations that are constraining its future possibilities.

A book must be more than just pages of paper bound together into a complete volume. Most people would agree that an alphabetical list of a city's inhabitants makes a different cultural contribution than Charles Dickens' *A Tale of Two Cities*. Without dismissing the importance of books of lists, the advent of computerised databases means that there is no compelling need to print and distribute; to publish them, as codex. Likewise, the hundreds of stocking fillers that take up counter space at bookstores. Those slender volumes with snappy titles (*How to Feel Good about Yourself without Hurting Small Furry Animals*) are not books in any meaningful sense. They are throwaway slogans; the 30 second ringtones of the literary world, that are essential to the now but add very little to the enduring sense of who we are. The world might need *The Green Day Book* (or whatever), but the sentiments involved, the ideas expressed could be scrawled on a greeting card, or sent in a bulk email with the subject heading 'you must read this'.

▶▶| Book culture?

Book culture is what distinguishes the book. Whilst the book emerged from the realm of print culture, it actually spurred a more sophisticated world view. The essence of the book is not grounded in Gutenberg and movable type. Instead it lies in ideals like the democratisation of ideas, of thinking and reflecting, of absorbing the thoughts of others, of creating one's own; of public conversation and discourse.

Book culture is centred on continuing the great human conversation through a process of writing, reading, editing and ultimately publishing *ideas*. This is very different from print culture, which focuses on the object that is printed. Print culture is as much about newspapers and magazines, brochures and leaflets as it is about books. Print culture can be motivated by a range of other factors; the need for publicity, the drive for profit. What cannot be denied is its reliance on a particular mode of delivery; that of printed object. On the other hand, book culture is not about books themselves; it is about the *process of interacting* with books. Of writing them, publishing them and reading them.

For a printed object to be a part of book culture, what characteristics must it have? Some, like Sven Birkerts, argue that the *literary novel* defines the book and that only such a genre allows the gentle immersion required for a book to truly communicate its ideas.[12] I'm somewhat less prescriptive. I think book culture can be more broadly defined. A book need not be literary, nor need it be a novel. To my mind, there are more important considerations.

▶▶ Ideas machines

A book must be an ideas machine. Whether its content is fiction or non-fiction, or it possesses the necessary conceits to be considered literary, or belongs firmly in pop culture sensibilities, it must contain ideas. They can be good ideas or bad ideas, concepts that you agree with or which provoke violent reactions such as banning or burning. Those views can be overt; stated upfront in bold print on page one, or subtly woven through prose of seeming irrelevance. They can be written elegantly and entertainingly, wrapped in a murder mystery with a classic three act structure and unveiled only when the protagonist resolves his innermost conflicts. Or they can be bullet-points, obvious propaganda without any delusions of storytelling. Irrespective of their worth or their expression, a book must contain ideas. Importantly, the book must attempt to *justify* the ideas it contains. If it does not, it is simply a pamphlet, a brochure spruiking the thinking of a madman. A book must make a case; either in substance or in rhetoric. It must try to convince its reader by weight of evidence or failing that, by its elegance. The test of a book's success doesn't lie in the value of its argument, but in its usefulness as an ideas machine; as a vehicle for communicating the ideas of its authors. PJ O'Rourke's ideas often grate. But damn he can be funny, and his books' worth can be located within that humour, in the very suggestion that liberals can't laugh as easily as conservatives.[13]

Whilst authors plant the seeds, it is publishers who nurture ideas. The book trade has traditionally been one where the ideas of authors have been caressed into existence by sympathetic publishers, keen to make a cultural difference. The role of publishers will be explored in more detail in Chapter 5. For now, it's enough to suggest that the nature of book publishing appears to have changed. Some write of a time when New York was a place where publishers and editors supported writers and their writing, so that the ideas could emerge.[14] For those of us engaged in writing and publishing in 2007, the memories can appear overstated, even mythical. Today's publishers do not publish books solely because their editors consider them to be important. There are other factors at work; and all too often, the need for a book to contain ideas is the *least* important requirement for publication. Instead, a book's short-term sales possibilities seem to dominate. So Paris Hilton gets the nod ahead of other titles. What's notable about such books is that whilst containing no idea between the pages, the idea behind the pages is blatantly obvious; exploit the celebrity in question in every media format possible. You've downloaded the video, now read the blow-by-blow. *Your Heiress Diaries* may be the product of print technology; it is part of the wider print culture. But it is not a book, but an anti-book and does not have a place in a book culture.

▶▶ Interactivity

But there is more. Melvyn Bragg's list of the great books[15] might include the *Football Association Rulebook*, but there are characteristics that books should possess beyond their social impact. And that is to do with how they engage readers. They must be *interactive*. Not in the point-and-click sense that new media mavens enthuse about, but in a way that causes readers to be engaged. Unlike the overt interactivity that the computer generation instinctively understand, books allow a more subtle 'internalised' interactivity that might be summarised in the Voyager Publishing Company's old slogan 'Bring your brain.'[16]

It's called *reading*. Readers use their cranial matter, kick their imaginations into gear or join the dots from within (and without) the text without the need for external prodding and poking. What I'll call 'internalactivity' is the thing that readers do when their brain meets the words and spaces on a page; it is what happens when they construct the meanings from those words and phrases, and then when they make the connections between those meanings and their own lives, their own world.

In fiction, this happens in the world of the imagination. James Bond's Bentley is pictured speeding down an English country road, and the reader can draw on his memory of that part of the country as well as Ian Fleming's description of the same. It is what happens when the reader consciously or subconsciously directs the action of the hero; reading more quickly in the scary bits, urging him on; more slowly in the parts of the story that have the hero luxuriating in the company of some exquisite creature or another. It is the links that the reader draws to other stories, already read, in which the hero has already acted a particular way; or even to imagined stories, scenarios that the reader dreams up on his own, using the characters and scenarios that have become so familiar. Mostly, this happens *inside*, invisible to the rest of the world, and is part and parcel of reading a book. Sometimes it is apparent to all; a child will play, acting out the roles of the *Famous Five* in turn; a teenager will draw on the elements of their role model heroes.

Non-fiction titles are the same; a good book will draw on its literary context; on other work done in the field, either overtly or subconsciously leading the reader to further exploration of the topic, other ways to satisfy their inquisitiveness. Readers of this book might be inspired to reflect on the arguments, and discuss them with their friends. They might follow the citation trail or remember another text that complements or contradicts the ideas within. But it's unlikely that a good book will provoke no reaction at all. Again, 'internalactivity' might happen invisibly, entirely in the mind of a reader, or it might involve running back and forth to the library shelf, hunting down footnotes and references. No matter. But a book allows, even demands this interactivity.

Part of which can be a certain sense of immersion. Birkerts argues that great books cause readers to enter a different mode, a 'meditative immersion that is, for me, one of the main incentives for reading'.[17] Whilst the sound and fury of a cinema experience drags the audience by the scruff of the neck into a darkened other realm and the newer media forms promise the virtual reality utopia of the *Star Trek* holodeck, the book has managed to entice readers into imaginary worlds with little more than words on a page. A good book allows a good reader to picture the protagonist, often causing them to imagine how their heroine looks or acts 'in real life'. How often has a film adaptation been criticised because the lead actor doesn't appear as imagined?

Readers disappear into their books, only to emerge when summonsed by their partners to the dinner table and the mark of a successful read is that tag line, so often thrown onto the cover by an overly-enthusiastic marketing manager 'I couldn't put it down'. The very best books often labour under the fate of a reader never wanting it to end. Whilst immersion in fictional worlds is superficially obvious, other genres have their own engaging qualities. Well-written prose has the ability to make biographies, histories or other drier topics come alive. Storytelling can cross genres; but the possibility of total enthrallment is an important facet of the interactivity that book culture demands; of what it is that makes a book.

Of course, 'interactivity' is one of those contentious new media words. Some argue that the problem with books is their *lack* of interactivity. Dale Spender[18] says that print culture is being displaced by what she calls digital culture (in which the authority of printed material is being replaced with the more conversational nature of the new media forms). 'Talking back', she argues, replaces being 'talked to'. It's an argument that holds water and one that I'm inclined to make myself; the appeal of the new media technologies is its potential for conversation, its possibilities of what Tim Berners-Lee (the inventor of the world wide web) calls 'intercreativity'.[19] All of a sudden, instead of finding ourselves in a lecture theatre, listening to so-called experts, we are in seminar rooms, working things out between ourselves. For some, new media represents the idealised public sphere, as conceived by German theorist Jürgen Habermas.[20]

But there is no single digital culture. It is complex. Drop into a chatroom, and the conversation can be banal, visit an academic mailing list and you'll see anything from thoughtful contributions to obscure cultural studies debates. Hang out at the wrong blog, and there'll be a thousand links to unverified celebrity sightings. Hang out at the right blog, and you'll find insightful observations about living in an occupied territory.

This isn't altogether a bad thing, and we should remember that Spender's digital culture reflects real life. Whenever people gather, different conversations occur. Put eight people around a dinner table, and it's mostly polite, and somewhat focused. Gather a hundred in a bar and clusters form. Couples pair off to flirt, those who know each other gravitate together, all the people wearing *Star Trek* t-shirts begin to talk and the rest watch the action silently clutching their drinks. So, there are conversations and there are *conversations*. Whilst it would be nice to think that all of our conversations possess the quality of a postgraduate seminar room, the reality is that most of our chatter more closely resembles a pub after a few too many drinks.

And that conversation is now faster than it has ever been. James Gleick observes how we now consume information at a far more rapid pace than previously. In *Faster*[21] he notes that we multitask. Flipping between two network shows, we watch the cable news services, a bit of MTV whilst surfing the web, leaping through dozens of different sites, browsing a magazine and instant messaging six buddies simultaneously. We are, he suggests, different creatures, able to absorb information far more quickly, to untangle complexity with more dexterity than our forebears. So television shows made 40 years ago appear simplistic and lack pace and we are able to digest an album review 'in 60 seconds'. And the plethora of internet-based media experiences seems to be designed to hold our attention for no more than 30 seconds or so.

Maybe the best way to define a book is as an expression of what might be termed 'deep thinking' that leads to 'deep conversation'. The key characteristic of book culture is that the ideas in a book have been well-considered, carefully thought through and crafted with some skill. Where Spender sees one-way communication through the likes of textbooks, I see one side of a *slower conversation*. A conversation that is essential if we are to properly understand the madness that is humanity. Book culture represents the 'deep and meaningful' conversations we need to have; a book is where humanity goes when it needs to reflect on itself and really think about those bigger issues.

And the culture extends beyond the book itself (irrespective of its material status); the wider conversation needs the book as a touchstone. The smalltalk, dinner party chat and pub arguments draw on ideas found in books, the wider conversation is at the very least informed by, and sometimes driven by book culture. As well as being an ideas machine, a book is a particular part of humanity's conversation. In print, this is easily seen. The diversity of print material encompasses the range of human discourse. Newspapers are a staple, as are the wealth of brochures, magazines, newsletters and flyers that represent the other chat that we indulge in; the gossip and innuendo, the water cooler banter, the argy-bargy of the public house. And books provide the substance to a conversation that not all people indulge in, but that all are affected by. Benedict Anderson identified newspapers and novels as the cornerstones for his 'imagined communities',[22] as key tools that allowed people to feel a sense of belonging to a particular identifiable community. In his argument, nations only existed because of a shared vision that arose because newspapers documented events that all could be concerned about and books expressed ideas about what it meant to belong. Readers assumed that there existed others just like them, simultaneously sharing the same media products, and by extension, the same cultural values. Thus nations were born.

Whilst newspapers might mark the daily passing, books are the actual minutes of each millennium; they record significant moments in ways that the ephemeral nature of other print forms does not. Rightly or wrongly, it is books that define our times. Even as the inevitable blurrings of fact and fiction, of time and place emerge with each written tome, book culture shapes the telling of our past. And perhaps much of this can be attributed to a culture of preservation that surrounds the printed book. The heft, weight, solidity and illusion of permanence that a book inspires encourages us to archive, or dare I say, hoard each and every one we own. Perhaps it's the cost, but whilst we happily toss copies of the daily newspaper (or the weekly gossip magazine) into the recycling bin once read, seldom are books treated so disdainfully. Despite the fact that few are read more than once. We are far more likely to pass a book on, or place it on a shelf where its only further use will be as an object to be dusted every few months, or packed into boxes for carrying from one house to the next. But because we hoard them, we turn to them for our history. I don't have the *Sydney Morning Herald* from 1973 celebrating the opening of the Opera House with a first hand account and vivid pictorial coverage. But I do have a book which records that moment in history. And it's clear that fiction comprises a huge component of our popular culture; either in book form, or as film adaptations. No cultural history of recent years would be complete without the defining elements of *Harry Potter* and *The Da Vinci Code*.

The bottom line? Just as book culture existed as a particular part of print culture, it also exists as a part of digital culture. If the internet is just 'people talking'[23] and allows the expression of an ongoing human conversation, then books represent *people thinking before talking*. Even in a prepubescent digital world, we turn to books for guidance and reflection. We look to considered ideas, well-thought out arguments and evidence-based analysis. Deep thinking still exists. Book culture still exists. More than that, we need it. We need the carefully considered ideas of those who are willing to devote the time and energy required to write a book.

Part of the deeper conversation is a notion of authority that books bring to the table; a concept that is in dispute as new ideas of authorship and content aggregation come into being. But we must not sneer at authority. Whilst some people (like myself) see the new media as allowing users to reject authority, expertise is still something that humans crave. What is different is how that authority is now conferred. In print culture, because publishing was expensive and rare, anything that appeared in book form had a gravitas that conferred immediate authority. Not so today. We're far more conscious of the fact that something in print does not deserve unquestioned respect. Instead, using the new media tools at our disposal, we have all become researchers and interrogators, and are likely to designate a source as authoritative only after it has been earned. But we still want – and need – some form of authority.

In book culture, the very act of properly editing a book demands that the book's ideas have been subject to some interrogation; that its prose has been refined and tuned to within an inch of perfection; that the hard questions that readers might ask of it have already been answered. The further act of publication requires that the context for the book's ideas are properly understood and the text is located in a place that will attract and appeal to as many people as possible, so that its authority can be tested in the wider marketplace of ideas.

▶▶ So, what is a book?

Underlying all of these components, this assemblage, is an abstract machine of sorts. An idea. What drives publishers to publish books? *What is a book meant to do?* Director of the Oxford International Centre for Publishing Studies, Angus Phillips, suggests that the object should no longer be privileged. Instead he argues that 'a book is what a book does'. He goes on to ask the question: 'What does a book do?'[24]

Throughout history books have performed various functions. They entertain, they educate, they instruct and inform. The reality is that in each of those realms, the book has been displaced. In entertainment, the book lags behind television, movies and other electronic forms. In education, the physical object is being displaced by a virtual one; encyclopedias, academic journals and textbooks are rapidly fleeing the realm of print. And in informing and instructing the world, the book is no longer the first port of call for many; the internet with its instant access has displaced the sombre authority of the printed word even there.

But it's easy to confuse the object of the book with its substance. A textbook delivered on a laptop screen it is no less of a textbook. A Yahoo! link to a chapter hosted on gutenberg.org is no less a book chapter. And just because *Bleak House* is on BBC1 instead of within the pages of a cloth-bound hardback makes it no less *Bleak House*. It is this blurring of boundaries that we must untangle; if the object of printed paper is no longer the key dimension of a book, then what is?

▶▶ It's about time

A book is not a *thing*; a book is a *process*. And what a book needs is time. Time to write and time to read. What distinguishes a book is the *premium of time* that it demands of both its authors and its readers. Notwithstanding the need to have a decent idea, something worth saying, writing a book is a time consuming process. Any author or would-be writer would tell you that, even if the words flow freely, it takes a long time to commit to the 40 or 50 thousand words that even a relatively short book requires. What's more, they can't be just any words, they have to be the right ones. The author needs to communicate effectively. Not only does she have to sustain a coherent argument over the course of hundreds of pages, but she has to conjure up words and phrases that make sense, and compel the reader to keep on reading.

It might be easy to write a few sentences, or several paragraphs, or the 2000 words needed for a serious magazine article. But a book is a further hurdle; it requires a commitment of time and resources that few people are in the position to make; or even desire to make. Which is probably why we think of books as special.

In addition, the time required to write a book affords authors the opportunity to dig a little deeper. Books are not compelled to react to current events with the same sort of urgency required of other media forms, allowing a more reflective and thorough approach. For example, in Bob Woodward's *State of Denial*, interview subjects were often more inclined to respond usefully to requests for information when they knew that their insights would not be relegated to 'the daily political sniping'.[25] It's hard to imagine that their insider perspectives would have been made available for anything other than a book.

Of course, other media forms demand huge investments of time. Feature films, music albums and videogames all involve casts of thousands, budgets of hundreds of millions and years to produce. Surely, they require a greater commitment than writing a humble book? Perhaps, but there is a difference. Most of the time devoted to making a film is spent constructing a reality from the director's imagination. Time is required to figure out *how to make the content visible*. Camera angles, lighting, how dialogue is emphasised by the actors involved. It takes months if not years to capture on film. The same for music and videogames. A modern multi-track recording studio allows for an infinite combination of production possibilities, which takes ages to explore. And in game production, render farms, storyboards, animation all take an enormous amount of both time and computing power. Again, they are resources required to make the creators' vision visible to the user. In a book, that work is delegated to the reader. Rather than create an epic battle scene with hundreds of actors, a picturesque New Zealand valley, and a production crew big enough to put man on the moon, all JRR Tolkien had to do was describe what was in his mind's eye. His readers did the rest; imagining details, painting pictures in their own heads using the words on the page as the basis for their work. Taking part in the interactivity that a book demands.

Instead of figuring out how to display the content, the author of a book uses her time to create that content; to think through the ideas involved, to pause and reflect on the storyline, the plot, the characterisations. Or in a non-fiction work, to frame arguments and find ways to make those arguments convincing. And even if the book is relatively short, its final form is a reflection of the energy involved in its creation; the sophistication of its content can be directly correlated to the effort put into its authorship.

Once a book is written, it's the reader's turn. A feature film might demand two hours; a novel often demands much more time than that. We might polish off a potboiler within a day, but most books take longer. And the more challenging titles; the ones which shake us from our slumber sometimes demand re-reading, and a commitment both in front of the page, and away from it that goes well beyond most other media forms. So it's no surprise that many people argue that they have no time for books. It's not just the hours, but the effort needed; and in this world of instant gratification, the requirement to set aside sustained periods to read and think is not high on personal agendas. Historically, the need for readers to *work* has come about because books are written in words, sentences that need interpretation; the interactivity that some say books do not have is present in the activity of reading. But limiting the definition of a book to words ignores other possibilities; where readers' minds must do work in other ways, possibly not yet imagined. Books are incomplete; words create a space that has to be negotiated by a reader in order to be meaningful. As John Carey in *What Good are the Arts?* suggests, 'a vital element in all literature is indistinctness ... The reader ... not only can but must come to some kind of accommodation with the indistinctiveness in order to take meaning from the text. For that, the imagination must operate.'[26]

Ultimately, books are about time; about slowing things down and forcing readers to slow down with them. Words don't come alive by themselves and readers need to get in synch with the pace of the writing, engage with the words as they come off the page and become a part of the conversation that the book is starting. It's not about printed pages bound and glued. It's about time. Books are to other media forms what cassoulet is to a Big Mac. And just as slow-cooked French provincial cuisine is not the same as pre-processed re-manufactured meat, book culture is different. It requires a more subtle manufacturing process, a less rigid recipe, a more intuitive method. And it demands more commitment from its readers. Just as cassoulet should not be scoffed with one hand whilst driving down an interstate highway, books should be savoured at length as is a fine meal. And the difference is rewarding. Those who choose to eat other than fast food or decide to read substantial titles find fulfilment in unexpected ways. It is life-defining, both as a process and an outcome. As a journey and a destination. Humanity's project is the better for books.

▶▶│   And the answer is?

Books are unlike newspapers or magazines or other printed media forms. They ask different questions of their readers than film and television ask of their viewers, or videogames do of gamers, or websites and blogs do of internet users. A book takes an idea and adds time. Months or years for an author to properly think through her text; an appropriate interval for a publisher to understand that text; a suitable period for a reader to engage with it. A book need not emerge as a trade paperback. A book need not be printed. It does not require the resources of a publishing company to manufacture an object, ship it around the world and store it in warehouses. It does not have to be expressed as words on a page. It may be words on a screen; or it may not be words at all. But it does require the peculiar form of interactivity which we call reading. And the problem is, nobody reads books anymore.

▶▶ CHAPTER 3.
Nobody reads

We are down to a gulag archipelago of readers. Of the sort of readers I've described, there are 176 of them in Nashville, 432 in Atlanta, 4011 in Chicago, 3017 in Los Angeles and 7000 in New York. It adds up to 60 000 people. I assure you there are no more.

Philip Roth[1]

Nobody reads books anymore. Not for entertainment. Nor for enlightenment. We have no time for the former, no desire for the latter. Our lives are too-short days filled with constant motion; we try to jam as much as we can into every waking moment. Nobody has the time to sit down and read an entire book; instead we multitask; we watch morning television over our weetbix and pilates, listen to podcasts during our commute, channel talkback radio and surf the web whilst putting together that powerpoint presentation at the office; catch *CNN* in the gym. We're busy paying off our mortgages and plasma TVs. And when we do get five minutes to relax, we sit down with one of a half dozen glowing screens; and choose from a Tivo'd episode of *Desperate Housewives*, a downloaded video of the latest Hollywood movie; a little *Halo 2* action, or a surf around defamer.com. Only in bed might there be time for a chapter or two of Dan Brown. And only if we haven't already fallen asleep.

We're watching *CSI* instead of reading novels and when we want to dig beyond the stories on the television news, we turn to the web. Books might still exist as touchstones for ideas, as things for the electronic talking heads to discuss. But fewer and fewer people read them; we rely instead on *Oprah* to do the reading and pass on the ideas within; or expect Google to turn up the appropriate search results.

Richard Charkin, CEO of Macmillan Publishers in the UK writes that 40 per cent of Europeans do not read books and in the developed world, more people use the internet for leisure than books. In the United States, the 2004 National Endowment of the Arts survey entitled 'Reading at Risk'[2] found that in 1992, some 60.2 per cent of the American population had read a book. By 2002 this had declined to 56.6 per cent. By the end of this decade, the trend suggests that less than half of the American population would have read a book during the course of the year. That's *a* book. A single book in 365 days. Australia is no different; reading books is not something that most of us do. The most recent Australian Bureau of Statistics time usage survey dates back to 1992, before the internet had made any mainstream impact. Even then, whilst the average Australian spent 103 minutes a day watching television, they spent all of seven minutes reading books.[3] Because some of us still read books for more than seven minutes a day, averaging out the numbers means that *most of us don't even do that.*

▶▶| But what is reading anyway?

Of course we are still *reading*. Most in the west are still literate and able to read and write more than competently. We're just not reading books. And there is a distinction between 'functional reading' and 'book reading'. At primary school, we're taught the former; my five year old reads her way through stories, working through increasing levels of difficulty, mastering the strangeness that is the English language; and there's an entire industry devoted to the important task of teaching kids how to read. As our education progresses to higher levels, we begin to explore different types of reading. We learn to read 'critically':

to interrogate the texts presented to us and negotiate their meanings usefully. And we also engage in 'literary' reading: the formal critiquing of a particular canon of works which will allow us to pursue the delights of being an English literature major. Somewhere along the line, reading becomes fun for some of us; the lure and escapism of a good story encourages us to pick up books for the sheer pleasure of doing so. And buried in that pleasure is the joy of playing with ideas and taking part in that great human conversation that book culture enables.

But most of us only read 'functionally': we read enough to get on with our everyday lives; train timetables, instruction leaflets for dishwashers and cookbooks; travel itineraries and home building contracts; department store catalogues and end user licence agreements. Sometimes functional reading extends to the information-gathering required to be *active* in a modern democracy: getting news and current affairs, figuring out our rights and obligations as a citizen and consumer. And sometimes it's work-related. It's the reading we have to do in our professional capacity, ranging from deciphering Objective-C programming manuals to doing research for high-school geography projects; keeping up-to-date with the *New England Journal of Medicine*, understanding the spare-parts catalogue in a car dealership or adapting the recipe for pad thai.

But reading is more than just literacy; it is not enough to recognise words and letters and make sense of sentences. Samuel Johnson was eighteenth-century England's most famous 'man of letters'; he gave the world his *Dictionary of the English Language* in 1755. But Johnson was, at heart, a functional reader. He considered 'true' reading to be motivated by the desire for information, or instruction. To Johnson, books were tools, carriers of knowledge, and he was keen to pursue wisdom through the printed word. But Johnson's idea of reading is not really book culture. After all, he once declared 'A book may be good for nothing, or there may be only one thing in it worth knowing; are we to read it all through?'4

Beyond this 'informational' reading is something else entirely; a reading that is fundamentally more ambitious. This reading is at once private and public; it is intensely personal (as Alberto Manguel's *A History of Reading*5 suggests) and because of that, has the potential to be world-changing. Reading is self-reflective, it is therapy for the individual reader; and a good book has the ability to do what nothing else is able to do. As Nick Hornby suggests, 'Books are, let's face it, better than everything else. If we played Cultural Fantasy Boxing League, and made books go fifteen rounds in the ring against the best that any other art form had to offer, then books would win pretty much any time...'6

But such reading is not easy. Book culture requires what novelist Zadie Smith calls a classical model of reading, one which casts the idea of the reader as an amateur musician 'who sits at the piano, has a piece of music, which is the work ... and they have to use their skills to play this piece of music. The greater the skill, the greater the gift that you give the artist and that the artist gives to you.'7 And it is this reading that no longer seems to happen. Few people immerse themselves in texts, and engage in that 'internalactivity' suggested in the previous chapter; they don't seem interested in *reading for its own sake*.

▶▶ Literary nonsense

Reading requires that the reader have a *readable book*; such a book is probably not defined merely by genre, but by intent. Of course, some genres lend themselves better than others to book culture. Some suggest that the literary novel is pre-eminent, and argue passionately in support of 'literature'. Sven Birkerts argues that 'literature holds meaning not as a content that can be abstracted and summarised but as experience. It is a participatory arena.' He goes on to suggest that

Through the process of reading we slip out of our customary time orientation, marked by distractedness and surficiality [sic], into the realm of duration. Only in the duration state is experience present as meaning. Only in this state are we prepared to consider our lives under what the philosophers used to call 'the aspect of eternity,' to question our origins and destinations and to conceive of ourselves as souls.[8]

John Carey concurs and declares that 'literature gives you ideas to think with. It stocks your mind. It does not indoctrinate, because diversity, counter-argument, reappraisal and qualification are its essence. But it supplies the materials for thought.'[9] Echoing Jean-Paul Sartre's notion of a committed literature, novelist James Bradley calls it 'super-fine fiction' and argues that literature is political, that 'serious writing ... refuses definition, refuses control and that is in itself a threat to many. One only has to watch the ferocity with which totalitarian regimes police the works of novelists to understand the threat the freedom of the page poses.'

Pretty heady stuff. And the reader of literature is becoming harder and harder to find. Bradley goes on to suggest that

Around the world sales are falling with alarming rapidity ... Where as late as the mid '90s novels still mattered, little more than a decade later, that urgency has almost entirely leached away, and the literary novel, like the literary novelist, has become, at least in every way our society takes seriously, irrelevant to the cut and thrust of modern life.[10]

Bradley is not alone. VS Naipaul and Norman Mailer are two more authors who fear for the future of the literary novel.[11] The American 'Reading at Risk' data doesn't distinguish 'literary' works in its rates of reading, but where the survey did enquire about rates of 'literary reading as well' (defined as 'novels or short stories, plays or poetry')[12] it found that only 46.7 per cent of the US population had read such a book in 2002, a decline from 54 per cent in 1992. Further most of those surveyed read between one to five books a year. The data suggested that only 25 per cent of Americans read six or more 'literary' books in 2002.

And sales data only confirm the readership surveys. UK figures suggest that in 2002, only 1.2 per cent of books sold could be defined as 'literature'.[13] In Australia, sales of Australian fiction fell from $205 million in 2001–02 to $73 million in 2003–04, with few such books selling more than 1000 copies.[14] Independent Australian publisher, Henry Rosenbloom suggests that 'in this country you can publish a very good novel and sell 700 copies'.[15] It's clear that printing literary books is not for the faint-hearted. In Australia, the independent publishers, Duffy & Snellgrove and Spinifex have ceased acquiring new titles; the academic presses are seeking to run at a profit; and the conglomerates are more interested in commissioning meaningless sure things.

As far as literary works are concerned, Philip Roth's estimates are probably correct. There are a handful of readers out there. Allan Luke in 'The Variability of Reading Practices' summarises: 'We constitute a particular aspect of book culture which has been described as that 10,000 who read literate "high cultural" texts ... and so forth.'[16] Luke suggests that there is no such thing as reading, but that 'maybe what we are dealing with is a family of related practices called readings, which ramify and multiply in various cultural sites according to different relations and different kinds of powers that be'.[17] His inference is clear; people still read, but the practice of literary reading is not common and whilst it may be privileged by some groups, it is no longer considered an *essential* practice. Governments, universities and other institutions appear to be more interested in functional reading; assuming that it provides more immediate economic value. The less tangible benefits of literary reading, of book culture may never show up on an accountant's ledger; making them less attractive to support. It's not just literature though. Another 'hard' genre is that of academic writing. Whilst career advancement still requires academics to write books, not many of them are being bought. Academic publishers regularly give examples of highly regarded monographs selling only 500 copies globally; partly because previously guaranteed sales to libraries have shrunk hand-in-hand with library budgets.[18] Nobody reads books anymore.

▶▶ But books still sell

If there are no readers, how come people are still buying printed objects called books? In 2005, the American book trade was a $35 billion industry.[19] Even Australians spent $1.35 billion on books in 2003–04.[20] Ignore the fact that they spent 10 times as much on gambling during the same period of time, and it's still a significant sum of money.[21] Break the big number down, and it's not so impressive. In Australia, it works out at about 130 million books sold.[22] It gets worse. About 50 million of those books are classified as educational;[23] for the most part textbooks and the like that students are *required* to buy. Take away those compulsory purchases and Australians bought 80 million books in 2003–04. Or about four for every man, woman and child.

It's probably useful to dissect those sales. For the sake of argument, I'm going to identify three (overlapping) categories: 'functional' books, 'anti-books' and 'books'.

A quick scan of the bestseller lists tells us a little about what books people buy. During the week that this was written, the top selling book in America was *You: On a Diet* by Michael F Roizen, in the UK it was *Guinness World Records* and in Australia *The CSIRO Total Wellbeing Diet Book 2*. Of course, bestseller lists are constantly changing and any particular week's figures might suggest different types of books are being sold, but the trends are pretty clear. People may still be buying books, but many of those books are not designed to be read from cover to cover.

Much of publishing caters for 'functional' reading – 'How-to' dominates the bestseller lists – cookbooks, dietary guides, cleaning tips, decorating titles, business books and self-help are what sells. The printed book seems to work well as a narrative-reference, in which the user follows step-by-step instructions, tempted by a tantalising glimpse of the piece's apparent climax and denouement. Full-colour pictures of passionfruit soufflés gently delude the average home cook and encourage him to join the dots in the accompanying prose.

But such titles don't privilege 'book culture', instead deferring to self-help culture or foodie culture. Functional books are ones that can easily exist in other media forms, and often do. The printed book is just one more vehicle for proselytising. They complement the multimedia elements that provide ample alternatives to the humble book; lifestyle television channels *show* the aspiring cook how to shred obscure tropical fruit in a way that 12 point Times Roman cannot convey. And the heady aroma of the finished product is made even more accessible with clever edits and cuts to 'one I made earlier'. Moving one's philosophical cheese might not yet be as telegenic as moving one's camembert, so self-help books don't appear to have the complementary presence of a pay television channel. Instead, such books are usually little more than an addendum to a speaking tour, spruiking some week-long motivational course for the price of a small used car. As ever, the book is merely one element in a broader multimedia marketing strategy; a necessary one, but seldom the centrepiece.

Also on the bestseller lists are a plethora of celebrity autobiography titles, and others intended to play to a particular moment in time. These anti-books might be designed to be read, but their existence owes more to sales potential than the quality of the ideas within. Anti-books are the boy bands of the publishing world, cynical creations, manufactured for marketing reasons only. These books make no lasting contribution to book culture. They may be print on paper, but they are no more designed to be *read* than a Toyota brochure. On the bestseller lists are titles such as the *Doctor Who: Official Annual*, the *Beano Annual*, Schapelle Corby's autobiography *My Story*, and *Why Don't Penguins' Feet Freeze?* One example (which practically defines the anti-book) that didn't make the bestseller lists after a moral outcry caused Rupert Murdoch to can its publication is OJ Simpson's *If I did it* (OJ's hypothetical take on his ex-partner's murder). Of course there will be arguments about which books are functional and which are anti-books. That goes without saying, but readers can generally pick what's what, and publishers know from the very beginning.

Take away those functional books and anti-books and we're left with books that are engaging and actually meant to be read. Whilst literature makes up a subset of such books, it is a very slippery thing to define. One man's literature is another's dead white prose. I grew up on a diet of mass-market blockbuster thrillers. Frederick Forsyth and Robert Ludlum were staples of my early teenage years, and despite its turgid prose, I couldn't put *The Da Vinci Code* down. So I think they're all books, even if the blockbuster approach to publication choice might mean that many publishers still focus on sales figures at the expense of quality writing. In short, this is not the place for a debate on the merits or otherwise of particular books. Instead, I'll suggest that if such a debate exists over a particular title, then it's probably contributing to book culture, and that title is therefore neither a functional book, nor an anti-book.

So the question that arises is not how many printed objects are sold, but how many books are sold. It's a hard question to answer, but in the UK in 2002, 30.3 per cent of books sold by volume were fiction titles. Children's titles made up 23.6 per cent, biography 6.2 per cent, literature 1.2 per cent and the rest were non-fiction genres ranging from food through to gardening. Without examining every title and its sales figures, a precise picture is hard to paint. But a stroll through a large bookstore would make it pretty clear – any way you slice it – a large proportion of the books that people buy are *not meant to be read*. At least not in the way that a book culture would understand reading.

▶▶   Books don't matter

There are, however, three sorts of lies: lies, damn lies and statistics. Which makes readership data a bit pointless, and nothing more than fodder for arguments over methodologies and apparent trends. For every survey which suggests that nobody reads, there is one that shows no real change in reading activity in the last couple of decades.[24] Sales figures can also be too opaque to be useful. But you don't need statistics to tell you which way the wind is blowing. A wet finger in the air can be more useful for a sailor than a hundred years worth of meteorological data. Irrespective of how many people are actually reading, even the most ardent booklover would admit that in the overall scheme of things, books are no longer particularly important. They simply don't matter.

As I wrote this chapter, two Australians died. One owned a zoo in Queensland and wrestled crocodiles on television. The other wrote over 80 books, one of which was made into a movie. One of those deaths was headline news all over the planet. The other received a short obituary buried deep in the capital city broadsheets. No prizes for guessing who received the most attention. It wasn't the author. In death, as in life, books are no longer the centre of our culture.

Whilst still breathing, Steve Irwin was more famous overseas than in Australia, where he was a recognisable and lovable, but hardly heroic rogue. He had a syndicated television show, appeared on *South Park* and *Jay Leno*, made a Hollywood movie and spruiked Toyota cars and the Australian Quarantine Service in his own irony-free way. Killed in a freak stingray accident, he became iconic; his death provoking an unprecedented global outpouring of grief. For 15 minutes, he was the most important person in Australia, and the most noteworthy Australian on the planet. Colin Thiele was a writer, the author of *Storm Boy*, a book about pelicans that was on Australian school reading lists for decades. The tale was made into a movie in the 1970s at a time when a proper Australian film industry was emerging. The day Irwin was killed, Thiele died of a heart attack at the age of 85. His death was as invisible as his life.

The contrast between Steve Irwin and Colin Thiele is stark; the global multimedia empire of the *Crocodile Hunter* still flickers on a billion screens as yellowing dog-eared copies of *Storm Boy* gather dust on school library shelves. And it reflects the broader reality. Books seldom matter anymore. Authors are no longer the font of all wisdom. Publishers are no longer the sole gatekeepers of knowledge. In the new world order, the book has been relegated to a distant last place. Our kids turn to Google or *The Discovery Channel* for information about killer stingrays. Or pelicans.

And desperate arguments to the contrary only emphasise this reality. A letter in a Sydney newspaper not long after both deaths underlined the disparity: 'The writer Colin Thiele ... died on the same day as Steve Irwin and his passing barely rated a mention, yet in a hundred years – when the name Irwin ... [is] forgotten – people will still be reading *Storm Boy*.'[25] Of course, it's an idea that's impossible to test right now, but 30 years after winning a Nobel Prize in Literature, how many of us are still reading Patrick White?[26] We'll look at this example in Chapter 5.

The political realm provides another case study; today's dispatches consist of sound bites on *Fox News*, pseudo debates and press conferences designed to manage spin as well as possible. The 2004 Australian federal election is a case in point. It was cast as a battle between an experienced incumbent prime minister in the form of John Winston Howard and a brash young pretender.

Mark Latham became opposition leader not long before the election and his star waxed and waned based on perceptions of his youth, his energy and apparent arrogant boofheadedness. Latham had a reputation as a head-kicker who was not afraid to call a spade a spade (or a conga line of suckholes) and who enjoyed the confrontational aspects of the political arena. In the media, he was portrayed as a bit of a thug who enjoyed the cut and thrust of a parliamentary stoush.

The fact that he wrote (and had published) several books was hardly mentioned; tomes which explored social and political ideas and which painted a picture of someone who was *perhaps* a little more thoughtful than many would wish him portrayed. A book culture might celebrate that fact, and use the books he had written to determine the measure of a man; his ideas could be dissected, his thinking understood. And because he had written a number of books addressing similar themes, the way his thinking evolved could be explored. All of which would provide valuable insight into the man who might be prime minister. Of course, none of this happened and very little attention was paid to Latham's books. Nobody appeared to read them. They may not have been very good,[27] but most people didn't even realise that he had written them. Nobody in the mainstream media reviewed them for the populace. No policy discussion was based on their contents. Those who were paid to absorb and disseminate news and opinions, the so-called political pundits didn't mention them. Their analysis was limited to sketchy sound bites and punchy grabs for the six o'clock news and the detailed policy thinking that might have emerged from the books in question was never undertaken. Even the man himself did not pay much attention to their existence. It was obviously felt that most people wouldn't care that he had written them; or worse would see it as a *negative*!

Ironically, since his defeat at that election and his subsequent fall from grace, Latham wrote a scathing memoir that *was* read.

More an anti-book than a book, it epitomised the 'fame-first' approach of publishers (and readers) who considered a warts-and-all bitch-fest far more worthy of attention than any attempt at laying the foundations for sound social policy.

▶▎ Have there ever been readers?

It is tempting to believe that book reading used to play a more prominent role in the shaping of cultures. Many gesture backwards in time to a golden era when books were the sole source of credible information, and their reading changed the world. James Bradley argues that novels once had the ability to change the world: 'Charles Dickens's *Nicholas Nickleby* played no small part in driving the reform of the Yorkshire schools in Britain, Doris Lessing's *The Golden Notebook* changed lives around the world, Ralph Ellison's *Invisible Man* was a touchstone for the US civil rights movement.' In *Amusing Ourselves to Death*, Neil Postman contrasts the reading habits of revolutionary America with the late twentieth century. In the 1700s, 'Reading was not regarded as an elitist activity, and printed matter was spread evenly amongst all kinds of people. A thriving, classless reading culture developed.'[28] Comparing the readership of Thomas Paine's 1776 *Common Sense* booklet (which sold between 300000 and 500000 copies) with a similar media event in the 1980s, Postman cites Howard Fast who suggests 'No one knows just how many copies were actually printed ... taking a figure of 400000 in a population of 3000000, a book published today would have to sell 24000000 copies to do as well.'[29] As Postman suggests, 'the only communication event that could produce such collective attention in today's America is *The Superbowl*'.[30]

The American Revolution might have been inspired by Tom Paine's printed pamphleteering and Benedict Anderson's imagined communities of nationhood might have been created by the double-barrelled print cultures of the novel and the newspaper. But by the late twentieth century, the community was imagined by media conglomerates, whose distribution mechanisms embraced the gamut of delivery technologies from cable and satellite television, radio networks, newspapers, magazines, cinema, and books.

Despite this, it is still debatable whether things were actually much different in the past. *Common Sense*[31] may have been widely read, but it is less a book than a well-considered pamphlet. Whilst its 16000 words demand more commitment than an episode of Larry King, it's a lot shorter than most books published today. And not much longer than some magazine pieces. For example, Joan Didion's article on Dick Cheney in a recent issue of the *New York Review of Books* runs to 8000 words.[32]

Moreover, there is a hint of elitism in championing Tom Paine; one might infer that because more people read *Common Sense* than (say) Barack Obama's *The Audacity of Hope*, democracy was somehow better in 1776 than in 2006. I suspect that many people, including Mr Obama might respectfully disagree.

John Carey laments an earlier time when 'in 1940 boys were reading about six books a month'.[33] Unfortunately, we don't really know what books they were reading, nor the circumstances of that literary act. Anti-books have been around a long time as well.

In New South Wales, the Premier's Reading Challenge requires school age children to read 20 books from a set list over seven months,[34] a rate of around three books a month. Whilst not quite Carey's celebrated rate of reading, many of the books on the set list are substantial novels. I'd say that gesturing back to a golden age of reading is seeing the past through rose coloured glasses; it's possible that reading always has been a marginal activity, and that book culture has always been lived by a minority of the population.

Two decades ago, William Goodman looked at readership figures through the prism of periodical sales. He identified magazines which 'serious readers buy', and examined their sales figures, with the caveat that 'Whilst this will not identify the actual readers of books, it does disclose the pool of those who may be expected to buy and read them.'[35] An interesting summary is as follows in Table 3.1.

Table 3.1: US magazine readership

	copies sold			copies per million people		
title	1872*	1954^	1983~	1872*	1954^	1983~
Atlantic Monthly	35000	201000	350000	921	1340	1522
Harpers	130000	154000	350000	3421	1027	1522
Nation	6000	31000	48370	158	207	210
New Republic	26000	30000	96606	684	200	420
Poetry	3000	3000	7000	79	20	30
Time	544000	1747000	4476504	14316	11647	19463
Life	1841000	5400000	n/a	48447	36000	n/a

* Population 38 million   ^ Population 150 million   ~ Population 230 million

While these numbers shouldn't be used as definitive arguments, it's clear that more general magazines (with shorter articles and fewer serious topics) like *Time* and *Life* sold (and continue to sell) in significantly larger numbers than those which Goodman suggests appeal to *readers*. He is forthright in his summation (reinforced by global sales of 38000 for the *Times Literary Supplement*): 'The relative decline in the capacity of serious literary and intellectual magazines to survive and flourish continues, or is at best only marginally better today than it was in 1872–1954.'

It is also clear that Goodman's 'pool of readers' has never been particularly big; the percentage of the US population that takes reading seriously *has always been a niche group*. He continues: 'I doubt that the percentage of the population interested in 'serious' books is any larger today ... than it was on October 7, 1929 when Faulkner's *The Sound and the Fury* was published. The first printing was for 1789 copies, a number, it was estimated, that would satisfy all demand for the book for nearly a year and a half.'

Goodman quotes Elisabeth Sifton, Viking's editor-in-chief who explains that

> The tiny readership for good books has remained fairly constant for decades, even as our population grows ... Bennett Cerf said forty years ago that selling 8000 copies of a book should make any publisher proud, selling 80000 was cause for celebration ... and selling 800000 was a positive miracle. That was true 140 years ago too, and it's about the same now. There is a natural limit on the readership for serious fiction, poetry and nonfiction in America that ranges, I would say, between 500 and 5000 people – roughly a hundred times the number of the publisher's and the author's immediate friends (Sifton's Law).[36]

So some people *are* readers, and most of them are women. Novelist Ian McEwan tried to give away some duplicate novels from his personal library. He went to the local park with his son and managed to give away 30 books in about five minutes. All but one of them went them to women.[37] And it's not only a fact of contemporary life. The novel and the woman reader appear to have grown up together.

Whilst the book dates back much further, the novel's roots can probably be traced to the 1700s. Whilst *Don Quixote* was a seventeenth-century precursor, many date the birth of the modern novel to the publication of Samuel Richardson's *Pamela, or Virtue Rewarded* in 1740. The following century saw the publication of many similar fictional narratives, built on realistic characters and events; something we can recognise as a modern novel. At that time, the readership was limited: 'Women of the upper and middle classes could partake in few of the activities of their menfolk, whether of business or pleasure

… Such women, therefore, had a great deal of leisure, and this leisure was often occupied by omnivorous reading.'[38]

From these beginnings, the novel became the domain of women. Martyn Lyons identifies the rise of new groups of readership that emerged from a suddenly literate culture in the 1800s. One key group of readers evolved from bible reading, in which women were the 'guardian of custom, tradition and family ritual'. By the twentieth century, 'for contemporary publishers, the woman reader was above all a consumer of novels'. Lyons argues that there was a 'feminisation of the novel reader' because

> novels were held suitable for women, because they were seen as creatures of the imagination, of limited intellectual capacity, both frivolous and emotional. The novel was the antithesis of practical and instructive literature. It demanded little, and its sole purpose was to amuse readers with time on their hands … novels, dealing with the inner life, were part of the private sphere to which 19th century bourgeois women were relegated.[39]

By the twenty-first century, the political dimension of reading has changed, but novels are still being read by women. McEwan suggests that 'reading groups, readings, breakdowns of book sales all tell the same story: when women stop reading, the novel will be dead'.[40] Go to any session of any writers' festival, and it's true. Men aren't interested. There may be a few of us attending, but the vast majority of festival attendees are women of a particular age. And even amongst women, there aren't that many readers.

▶▶| What's wrong with books?

Why don't people read books? Because they are too hard, too heavy, too long, too expensive. Largely irrelevant. In the fast-paced information age, the printed book is to digital what the

Queen Elizabeth II is to a Boeing 777. On an Atlantic crossing, the stately ship from Southampton provides more of a sense of occasion; it gestures to an age when travel was an event involving dinner suits and captains' tables; it avoids jetlag and is ultimately more fulfilling than hopping into a padded tin-can hurtling blindly through the sky at 10 miles a minute. But for most people, five hours compared to five days is no choice. Nor is a few hundred dollars compared to a few thousand. For functional reading, there are good alternatives to books.

The great fear of many during the 1970s and 1980s was that reading culture would be replaced by visual culture; that the role of books and newspapers would be taken over by movies and television. And to a large extent, those fears have come to pass. Electronic media forms dominate our culture. The 1990s brought a new mode of engagement. Bill Gates called it the 'web lifestyle';[41] the first place we now turned to when we needed information, or entertainment was the internet, through the world wide web. When first mooted, such a conceit was laughable, but as the new century dawned and an entire generation did exactly that, the idea of a web lifestyle is no longer confined to geekdom. Its unintended consequence is a return to reading. Despite attempts at multimedia, audio and video, the great bulk of web content is text-based. It's words, words and more words. In the '80s, teenagers watched episodes of *Knight Rider* on network television. Today they do the same on YouTube, only it's surrounded by commentary and discussion on the relative merits of David Hasselhoff.

The other possible consequence of a web lifestyle is a shift in reading culture, how people are reading. Jakob Nielsen wrote the definitive guide to web-writing in the early 1990s, which he called *Concise, Scannable and Objective*.[42] The web exaggerated a trend already apparent in our increasingly time-poor society. People haven't stopped reading, but they are reading differently. Instead of devouring huge slabs of text in one sitting, they tend to scan and sift, preferring bite-sized chunks and shorter pieces to longer prose. There's a perception that we can no longer sit still long enough to concentrate on anything meaty. As well, there's a feeling that young people in particular possess some form of attention deficit disorder, and publishers seem to pander to this apparent shorter attention span. For example, it is constantly suggested that newspaper pieces aren't as long. Lengthy magazine articles – once a staple of 'quality' publications – are no longer common.

The editor of *Maxim*, a magazine with a readership of nearly 11 million (mainly male) readers suggests: 'Our readers ... have shorter attention spans than any previous generation, they are chronically over-stimulated and easily bored.'[43] The editor of *Rolling Stone* agreed, saying that 'People just don't have as much time to read.'[44] Indeed, the number of people under 35 reading newsweekly magazines and long-form titles such as the *Atlantic* essentially halved between 1986 and 2002. Moreover, when they did pick up a copy, they spent less time reading it. In 1990, 18–24 year olds spent 43 minutes reading an issue; in 2002, it was 29.[45]

Our instincts would suggest that the pace and constant demands of modern life mean that we no longer have the time to read – or do anything else – for any decent length of time. In between working hours and traffic jams, bank queues and time spent on hold we barely have time for a microwaved dinner in front of the *Daily Show*.

But some research suggests that these instincts are wrong; longitudinal data from a University of Maryland research project shows that free time has actually *increased* over the last half of the twentieth century. In 1965, Americans averaged 36 hours of free-time a week; in 1995, it was 44.[46]

It seems that we have more free time, but we also have considerably more choice in our leisure-time activity. There are more television channels, books, movies, and music. And the internet has almost made the conquest of time and space possible. You can obtain most anything, anytime. Try YouTube for that old episode of *Gilligan's Island*. Or check your favourite online music store to find the Bee Gee's greatest hits. The dazzling array of possibilities forces us to spend less time on one particular activity.

Even within the confines of print, significantly more titles exist from which to choose. The introduction of desktop publishing technologies with their comparatively low cost and ease of use have spawned a magazine for every interest under the sun. The world wide web increased even that selection by an order of magnitude. It was suddenly possible for *everybody* to publish. Which is something we'll tackle later in this book.

For the moment, let's consider the other consequence of the web lifestyle as a shift in delivery medium. Reading words on a screen is no longer anathema to many; and in some sectors the possibility that print may no longer be the delivery medium of choice is openly mooted. The British Printing Industry speculates that the market for printed magazines in 10–15 years' time may be 40 per cent of current values and identifies TV listings and business magazines as areas where print versions will disappear within five years.[47] Even traditional publishers are testing the waters. *New Yorker* magazine has made its entire archive available for sale; that's every page of 4000 issues from February 1925. Only, it's not being published on paper, but being sold as a set of nine DVD-ROMs, or installed on a portable hard drive.[48]

And it seems that print newspaper readership is in decline, with many now getting their news from the world wide web. Research suggests that many younger readers feel that the newspaper *as an object* is wasteful and inefficient. The next generation apparently doesn't understand the whole concept of the printed newspaper:

There's a reader lurking in the greater Washington region who's haunting news executives at the *Washington Post*. He's a youngish man, a recent law-school graduate. When presented with a copy of the *Post*, this fellow fumbled with it, according to sources. He professed that he didn't know how it was organized. And the kicker: He expressed wonderment at the spread known as the editorial/op-ed pages. How could this well-educated man be so clueless about his local newspaper? Well, he's not. He reads the Post constantly on its Web site, WashingtonPost.com – 'sometimes for a few minutes, sometimes for hours,' according to a Post source.[49]

Piers Morgan, former editor of the *Daily Mirror* suggests:

End of story. Within five years every newspaper will be free and they'll all be online. And if they're not, they should be. There will still be a presence in print but that will be for older readers and you will find that anybody under the age of 35 will only read newspapers online.[50]

People are still reading newspaper content; they're just not reading newspapers. The book has not yet reached that nadir. Whilst newspaper readers are happy to peruse short articles while sitting at (largely) fixed computer screens, far fewer people appear to be willing to indulge in the reading of longer texts on the same screen. For the moment.

The bottom line is that we are starting to see a shift in our reading habits; in both *how* we are reading and *what* we are reading. For both our functional and our fun reading, we are faced with a plethora of choice and turning away from print on paper sources. We are dipping into more material, but spending less time with each selection. All of which suggests that reading books – those paper-bound objects that demand time, attention and concentration – is no longer a widespread cultural habit. We turn to them less and less for functional reading (with newer technologies such as databases, navigation systems and the like providing more efficient information solutions). And we appear to be turning to them less and less for fun.

Tim O'Reilly (founder and CEO of O'Reilly Media, a prominent computer book publisher) makes the observation that books compete with other services.[51] So, reference books don't necessarily compete with other reference books, but with search engines such as Google. And *Harry Potter* novels don't necessarily compete with other escapist teen fiction, but with entities such as *World of Warcraft*. In short, there are now alternatives to books. The printed book is the ocean liner of information sources. Indulgent, luxurious, romantic, exquisite to touch, a pleasure for all of one's senses. But compared to the attractions of other information sources, it is too slow, expensive, and belongs in another era.

Sure, books might appear to be cheap. But it's part of our psychology to underestimate our spending when we do it in small units. Buy a book a week at $20 a throw[52] and pretty soon you've paid for a large screen television. And once the screen is paid for, television is almost free; even basic pay television costs little more than a paperback a month. The same for broadband internet. In my household, there are thousands of books. Some are on shelves, some stored in boxes waiting to be properly unpacked and organised. Not one of those books cost less than $10 – most would have been closer to $30, some a whole lot more – the money we've spent on books approaches the price of a new family car. Books, like it or not, are not cheap; they are a significant investment. As John Sutherland suggests in *How to Read a Novel*: 'Novels are expensive to buy. Their new, hardcover, price has consistently been between 5 and 10 per cent of the UK national average weekly wage over the last two centuries. They are also expensive to produce and distribute.'[53]

And book buyers are as cost-conscious as anyone. Book sales in Australia decreased steadily between 1978–1989, which some attribute to a 'sharp increase in book prices relative to

CPI'.[54] Notwithstanding the presence and use of public libraries, buying books has always been a fairly expensive pastime. In fact, book reading began as a fairly elitist occupation. The cost of books in the eighteenth century was largely prohibitive to all but the relatively wealthy. Ian Watts in 'The Rise of the Novel' tells us 'The prices of novels, then, though moderate compared to larger works, were still far beyond the means of any except the comfortably off.'[55] It was only the invention of the paperback that allowed reading to reach the masses. But today, even that humble paperback is a relatively expensive habit.

There might be a couple more reasons why people don't read books; both of which are as much about perception as reality. Firstly, they look like hard work. A book requires commitment from a reader and only those who have experienced the satisfaction of a good book will choose to do the work over the promise of instant gratification. Chicken nuggets may be easy to eat because they don't require chewing, but they are ultimately less satisfying that a real roast chicken. But when we're hungry, we tend to reach for the most convenient fare. To many, reading a book is *work* (as is cooking a chicken), not something done for pleasure; the rewards seem too far away.

Secondly, the interactivity of a book is invisible. We tend to want to do something with our time; reading a book seems passive and not engaging. Of course, readers know better. But ask a 12 year old boy to choose between their Xbox and a collection of *Stormrider* novels and I suspect that you'd be eBaying the books, not the Xbox. It's not that young people can't concentrate for long periods of time (just watch two teenagers play *Halo* for an entire weekend); it's not that they don't read (they do, it's just not printed books); it's not that they don't write (texting counts, as does blogging and email); it's not that they're not interested in ideas (or at least any less so than any other younger generation); it's just that books aren't sufficiently attractive.

On the one hand, the sheer passivity of television is perfect for 'doing nothing'. Nothing beats the up button on a television remote control for providing just enough stimulus whilst in a vegetative state. At the other end of the engagement scale, video games provide an entrancing experience, and the opportunity to live temporarily in a little parallel universe. And there's also the internet, with its infinite possibilities for exploration and opportunities to engage in a never-ending conversation about, anything really.

In this universe, the immersive, interactive enticements of the book are just too subtle. *Readers* know that a good book possesses that certain something that can make it the perfect entertainment option. But not that many readers exist. All those others, rightly or wrongly, perceive books to be dull, static, unengaging, and less than dynamic.

For anyone brought up with a twenty-first century digital mindset, the printed book is an anachronism; books are everything that the new media technologies are not. There is no motion, there is no noise. There is no way to interact with the characters or the story. There is no-one else involved. Reading is a solitary experience. You can't talk back. It's just you and the words on the page. And all you can do with those words is read them; apparently there is no other way to engage. For a generation raised on newer media forms, the apparent one-sided conversation of a book defies logic. Elle Macpherson[56] is reputed to have asked 'Why read something that you haven't written yourself?' In the age of the world wide web, chat rooms, MySpace, Yahoo! Messenger, IRC and SMS the question might be 'Why read, when you can write?

▶▶ CHAPTER 4.
Everybody writes

There are no true readers today, only would-be writers.

Gore Vidal[1]

A friend of mine recently won *The Australian*/Vogel Literary Award for new fiction. Sponsored by a bread-making company and a newspaper, the Vogel rewards the unpublished work of young Australians under the age of 35. (It's nice to know that 35 is still considered young by *someone*.) As a launching pad for a literary career, winning the Vogel is a pretty good place to start. Far from being a repository of one-hit-wonders, many of its winners have gone on to publish widely and successfully.[2] Every year, the Vogel receives around 200 entries, of which a handful are shortlisted by the judging panel of three. The winner gets her novel published, pockets some cash and gains the kudos of her peers. Everybody else receives pretty much nothing. Such is the nature of book publishing.

Apart from the litcrati, nobody seems to notice the Vogel. It might rate a mention in the quality broadsheets, but that's about it. A quick check of the Australian Publishers Association's bestseller list doesn't show any recent winners. Which means that in 2004–05, no Vogel winning book sold more than 10000 copies. Maybe Gore Vidal was right; more people want to win the Vogel than read its winner.

▶▶ From writer to author

Everybody is a writer. Once written, getting a book published is the holy grail. *Getting published* represents a validation of sorts, a sign of approval. If a publisher prints it, it must be good. Getting a book sold is another thing entirely. And getting a book read is probably the most difficult thing of all.

We teach our kids to read, to write and to do math. From an early age, 'writing stories' is central to their education; even as the more creative pursuits of primary school evolve into the writing of more formal reports. What's more, the study of literature, of how stories are made and what they mean is central to our learning. So it shouldn't be surprising that everybody fancies themselves a writer.

Most writing is invisible. Secret journals are filled with adolescent angst, half-written novels lie dormant in desk-drawers, never to be seen by anyone, 20-somethings spend their days writing self-absorbed attempts at contemporary classics. The occasional effort is made public; sent unsolicited to an agent or a publisher only to end up in a slush-pile in the corner of an editor's office. Even more occasionally, a manuscript is published. At that point, when a book emerges from the unsolicited pile; or even when a commissioned book becomes a real object, something happens. When the book launch is done, and the book sits on shop shelves to be turned cover-out by family and friends, a writer becomes an *author*, they have been accepted into an elite club, their chosen path has been validated. Wanting to be an author is the sign of a healthy ego, a way of *trying to convince yourself that you matter.*

Books provide the vehicle for those who wish to become authors. Getting a book published, with its institutionalised culture of approval, was for years the only way in which writers could become authors. The path to authorship was known; write a book, submit a manuscript to an agent or a publisher, and then get published. The difficulty in negotiating the various hurdles required to evolve from a writer into an author only made the rewards of authorship more attractive.

Modern publishing, however, appears to have different priorities. Publishers seldom draw on unknown writers; some no longer have a so-called slush pile and many publishers no longer accept unsolicited manuscripts. Too much work is required to read them and decide what is publishable; it is often easier and more profitable to make books another way. So books are commissioned based on ideas pitched from within or from agents. Ideas which are themselves based on what is thought might sell. Today, authorship is not something a writer earns by being published, but something bestowed on whoever has a saleable idea.

Roland Barthes wrote a eulogy for authors in the mid-1960s. His 'Death of the Author'[3] famously separated the author from her text, any role in the *reading* of that text, and from her reader. His compatriot, Michel Foucault, clarified the purely functional role that an author might play. To him, the author served a *classificatory* function, which can be seen in the way that libraries and bookshops are organised. Beyond Dewey Decimal or genre, it's almost always done by the *surname of the author.* (And given the sales advantage of being at eye-level to the potential buyer, authors have apparently been advised to change their names to maximise their exposure.)[4] The 'author function' is also about attribution; about conferring authorship to a particular person, or persons. As a result, it is tied up with the law; the author bears a responsibility for her words, and is consequently granted the rewards borne of that responsibility. And the author-function is about branding. Very few book buyers understand the role of publishing imprints and generally buy books by particular authors, irrespective of their publisher. Just like brands of running shoes or jeans, the author-function is about marketing and reputation. The brand must be properly *spun*, it must be managed for best advantage; as surely as the mythology of the wild west has no bearing on today's made-in-Vietnam Levis 501s, the author-function need not actually resemble an actual author in any way whatsoever.

Part of the problem is that there are far more author wannabes than publishing companies want to deal with. Rather than finding writers and nurturing their ideas, this wealth of writers has allowed book publishers to take a completely different approach to publishing. Because they're concerned with shifting objects rather than ideas, the motivation for publication is not the quality of the writing, nor the idea. Instead publishers rely on a hook (not a book) that allows their sales team to properly pitch the book to booksellers in the 15 seconds or so they have to make the sale. That hook can be a movie tie-in, a comprehensive merchandising campaign, previous success as an author, or earlier fame at just about anything. In an age where everyone writes and nobody reads, writers will inevitably struggle to be heard above the din. An opinion piece in the *Sydney Morning Herald*, written by an author wannabe with a collection of rejection slips summed up the problem:

> unknown writers stand no chance against known non-writers. Let's face it: if I want to get published I'm going to have to become famous for something else first. I need to survive something against incredible odds, or commit a serious crime and endure a brutal stretch of incarceration, or sail solo around the world for no reason.[5]

So in an age when everybody writes, the way books are made has been inverted. No longer is it necessary to begin with the writer; now publishers can begin with the book. A publisher might come up with an idea like a cookbook, or an illustrated book about dinosaur fairies, or a book on the death of the book. And then find someone famous to write it. Because everybody writes, writing is a commodity. And the law of supply and demand holds true, publishers are swamped by writers demanding to be published, so for the most part can control the market for written goods.

▶▶| New media, new writing

If the book publishing industry was the *only* means of production, this would be a problem. But, as ever, the internet has acted as a social amplifier. Not only has it provided a means of production to millions of writers, it has turned them into *authors* with significant readership. No longer is a publishing company required to validate their ideas and expression. Instead, they are tested in a live marketplace of ideas. On the web, every step from writer to author occurs in public: a writer's reputation is immediately up-for-grabs; their validation or otherwise is accessible, instant and visible to anyone with a connection. Is it different from print on paper publishing? Yes. But, crucially, in the paperless world of the new media, you don't have to be a Vogel winner to matter.

Perhaps the key characteristic of the new media is a shift in emphasis from consumption to production. New media does not have audiences but users; or in the parlance of some, it has 'producing consumers' or 'prosumers'. Of course, there are still distinctions between people we call writers and people we call readers, but there are undoubtedly more avenues for publication. As a result, more people *can be seen* writing and creating.

Tim Berners-Lee's 'intercreativity' (see Chapter 2) is a key characteristic of the internet; one which distinguishes it from older media forms.[6] In this new world, everyone is encouraged to be a creator of content, as an author, photographer, musician or film-maker. Angst ridden teenagers no longer confide their deepest secrets to their diaries, now they can 'show and tell' to the world. That special wedding video is no longer only for a treasured group of family and friends. It can be youtubed and googled, so that even the most far flung non-relatives can find it and watch it.

The internet makes the invisible visible. Whereas previously our frothings about the latest Dan Brown novel have been drowned in schooners of beer at the local, now we can post our impressions to Amazon's reviews. Our long hidden angst over the worth of the *Lord of the Ring*s movies can be published on the Internet Movie Database. The internet allows users to respond to media products and contribute to ongoing discourse. And as well as critiquing media products, we are *reinventing* them. For example, fan websites or newsgroups allow devotees to obsess over *Buffy* or *Lost*. They can chat at length with like-minded peers, and speculate on characters and possible outcomes. And they can create entirely new plotlines based on characters from their favourite soap opera or sci-fi series. This 'fan fiction' allows audiences to redirect the outcomes of their favourite shows to their own liking, and publish it for peer acclaim or rejection. The fanfiction.net website is one such repository of parallel universes. It lists thousands of shows, with literally millions of alternative storylines. For example, the last time I looked, there were thousands of scripts for *The West Wing*. This was only one of many media products evolving in the hands of its audience in ways its creators may not have intended.

MIT professor and cultural critic, Henry Jenkins argues that fan fiction is a way for users to re-take control over their myths. He suggests that:

> if you go back, the key stories we told ourselves were stories that were important to everyone and belonged to everyone. Fan fiction is a way of the culture repairing the damage done in a system where contemporary myths are owned by corporations instead of owned by the folk.[7]

Away from these mashed-up media products, there are those who write from scratch, who publish their own writings on the net; anything from new recipes for snail porridge to reviews of the best Peking Duck restaurant on the planet; from political analyses to examinations of the latest cool running shoes. As many have noted, publishing on the web is not difficult. And indeed, many are writing of books; using their web presences to review new releases, comment on the industry, suggest titles to like-minded readers. Authors too are slowly embracing the possibilities. Some, like Jeanette Winterson are fulsome in that embrace.[8] She has a substantial web presence, offering an archive of various writings, extracts from new books and the possibility to engage with the author in her forum. Others are less enthusiastic, but whether book people take advantage of them or not, the new media forms have at the very least provided new ways for writers and readers to connect.

►► Blogs: instant global publishing

Now, everyone blogs. Whilst webpages are simple to create, a barrier still exists; you have to think (just a little bit) like a programmer to build a website. Despite the small size of that hurdle, it is real enough to prevent many people from publishing on the web. Blogs changed all that. Blogging tools are as easy to use as email, and importantly, cost nothing. Type your words, press a button and your blog is updated. Like it or not, blogging is either your worst nightmare, or your ultimate dream: instant global publishing.

Most blogs are chronological; *time* is the key dimension for their creation and continual updating. Every entry is time and date stamped, and listed in reverse chronological order. There is normally a calendar with days highlighted signifying the presence of a post, so the nature of blogs is to demand of the blogger constant, regular postings and it's commonly accepted that the most popular and influential blogs are the ones that are updated regularly. Furthermore, the technology has evolved to allow easy tracking of a blog's progress. Tools such as RSS (Really Simple Syndication) feeds alert blog readers that their favourite blogs have been updated, obviating the necessity to visit a blog unless new content has been added.

For those concerned about 'quality', there are mechanisms for assessing the worthiness of blogs. Unlike traditional publishing, there is no editorial board or acquisitions meeting. Instead, a blog's visibility is constantly judged in real-time by its readers. By counting trackbacks (or other blogs which link in), recommending and tagging in social networks like digg.com or del.icio.us, and allowing open commentary on blog posts, an environment has emerged which rivals the traditional publishing institutions. Blogs might not be copyedited or peer-reviewed. But their success depends on another mechanism entirely; validation depends on what the readers think. Get it right, and technorati.com will rank your blog highly. Get it wrong, and it will disappear from the radar. Of course, the words will still exist somewhere on the world wide web. But they will cease to matter.

As a result of this transparency, the 'blogosphere' has exploded in scale and possible influence. There are tens of millions of blogs out there, a number which doubles every six months. And the diversity of blog topics reflects that of the internet's inhabitants. They range from highly personal commentaries on specific topics to broad-brush forums for political diatribe. Some of these are read by huge numbers of people. The bigger blogs such as instapundit.com or boingboing.net are visited by up to *half a million* people a day.[9] In brief, the blogosphere is changing how we read and write and it provides ample evidence that media consumers *are* becoming media producers. Blogs are filling a need; a desire for writers to be published and validated in some way.

▶▶ But a blog is not a book

If you believe the booklovers, most of what's on the internet is crap. In a panel discussion, Australian publisher Mark MacLeod fired off the standard refrain about the lack of editing on the internet suggesting 'the best thing about the Internet is that anyone can post something, which is also the worst thing about it'.[10] Well, maybe. Just because something is on the internet does not make it worthless, and rather than dismissing a text because of where it's found, publishers might find inspiration, or even material in that unlikely place. The very fact that so many people are writing and reading blogs shouldn't be ignored.

Still a blog is not a book. Blogs are to books what a riff is to a complete symphony. Naturally, there's room for both riffing and symphonies. And whilst a riff might lead to a masterpiece, a riff is not enough. Beyond the riff, the music can also break down in a cacophony of clichés. A blog's emphasis (some might suggest preoccupation) with timeliness runs counter to those things which I have identified as essential to book culture. Blogs are seldom slow, thoughtful and reflective, although they can be. More commonly, they represent short periods of intensive thinking, writing and posting. This is reflected by the time people spend reading blogs. Half a million might read dailykos.com every day, but they probably don't spend much time there. Surveys suggest that the average reader spends little more than a minute or two reading the average blog.[11]

But whilst blogs do apparently pander to those with shorter attention spans, it's worth noting that there are other possibilities inherent in their construction. Most blogs are non-destructive; they are added to and archived. Unlike newspapers which we tend to throw away at the end of each day, blog content (like all digital media forms) takes up almost no space in the living room and so is seldom discarded.

What blogs *can do* is represent a cumulative wisdom; whilst individual posts can sometimes appear banal and less than enlightening, a collection of posts over a period of time can have a more significant impact. So a blog can evolve into a more substantial text. For example, it's possible to see blogging as live drafts of a finished product; as viewing what used to be invisible in the writing process; as a hidden camera looking at the process of a writer becoming an author.

Enter the 'blook', a hybrid text that began life as a blog, and ended up as a printed book. In 2002, Salam Pax was the so-called blogger from Baghdad whose daily musings on life in that city prior to the current Gulf War was essential reading for many. The *Guardian* tracked down the anonymous author of the blog and published his writings in book form.

In Australia, Margo Kingston's Webdiary was an area of Fairfax Digital that Kingston ran as her own fiefdom. It has since shut down after a dispute with her publishers, but during its lifetime, Kingston encouraged contributions from writers across the political spectrum and took up political themes drawing on a range of ideas and opinions. Webdiary, according to its charter existed:

> to help meet the unmet demand of some Australians for conversations on our present and our future, and to spark original thought and genuine engagement with important issues which effect us all[12]

A book entitled *Not Happy John* published by Penguin in Australia emerged out of Webdiary. Whilst 'authored' by Margo Kingston, the book featured writing by Antony Loewenstein, Jack Robertson, Harry Heidelberg and Hamish Alcorn, all of whom had been regular contributors to Webdiary. By the middle of 2004, Penguin had printed 29000 copies including a couple of reprints, and the book was a non-fiction bestseller around Australia.

More recently, print on demand publishers, lulu.com created the Blooker Prize with fiction, non-fiction and webcomic categories.[13] The 2006 winner of the non-fiction prize was *Julie and Julia: 365 Days, 524 Recipes, 1 Tiny Kitchen Apartment*. The book started as a blog in 2002 as an attempt to tell the story of Julie Powell's attempt to cook all of Julia Child's recipes. The blog developed a wide audience, and the author drew on their feedback in the writing process: 'the blog readers were almost in a way co-writers – certainly inspirations'.[14] The blog gained media attention and was eventually published as a book by Little Brown, selling more than 100000 copies. *Julie and Julia* is not the only blook success story. *Baghdad Burning,* a blook by an anonymous Iraqi author was longlisted for the 2006 Samuel Johnson Prize for Non-fiction.

Many more titles have since emerged from this possibly fertile, yet non-traditional soil. High-profile 'crossovers' include Stephanie Klein, Jessica Cutler and Ana Maria Cox. Klein's greek tragedy blog landed her a $500 000 publishing deal with Regan Books (a HarperCollins imprint) which resulted in *Straight up and Dirty: A Memoir*. Cutler's online Washintonienne diary became a novel of the same name and Cox's contribution to the Wonkette blog parlayed into the printed novel *Dog Days*.

The jury is still out on how successful 'blooks' are. Indications so far suggest that some publishers jumped aboard the blog-to-book bandwagon, assuming that having a blog provided an author with a ready-made readership. Some were disappointed when this market-driven approach did not succeed.[15] A more considered approach would understand blogs as nothing more or less than the very public evidence of the fact that everybody writes. So far, book publishers have tried to exploit a blogger's perceived popularity, in the hope of shifting objects (anti-books, perhaps?) in a bookshop. So the emphasis has been on converting the medium of publication from screen to paper. In the longer term, it might be more useful to ignore the *medium*, instead focusing efforts on helping writers become authors; and creating content that matters.

▶▶| What print can't do

The problem for book publishers is that they have little experience in some of the more interesting stuff that is being created. The only context they have is that of the printed object; and so their new media activities continue to gravitate towards that object. Instead of exploring opportunities beyond the printed book, they argue over 'electronic rights', as if there is a natural segregation between content on paper and content everywhere else. Which there is not.

The web does not contain only words, but consists of a myriad of media forms, all with their own possibilities; from games to videos, from animations to hypertexts. It's just possible that some of this stuff will matter; that soon, some of the ideas that are pitching around the network will take on significance beyond a viral email chain. And that some of it will inhabit what I call book culture more comfortably than most printed books do. The problem for those wedded to print is that many of these new developments *cannot exist as a printed object*; even those that are primarily based around words.

The new media forms allow for dynamic collaborative writing possibilities; live sites of information and engagement that just aren't possible in print. The most common example is the wiki. A wiki is the ultimate collaborative writing venture. It is web-published content that all users are welcome to add to and edit; a methodology that instinctively suggests chaos. The reality is otherwise. The collective intelligence of the readership (usership?) is put to good use as the accuracy and usefulness of the content is constantly tested and verified.

The most cited example of a successful wiki is Wikipedia, an online encyclopedia created by voluntary collaboration. This relatively recent creation employs no researchers or writers; it does not 'publish' in the traditional sense, but instead provides a venue for everyone to contribute their expertise. In a democratisation of both reading and writing, Wikipedia provides an alternative to the publishing norm of top-down publication with annual updates, cross checked by teams of experts. Instead, it is continually updated, its entries constantly corrected by users who come across errors in fact or simply timeliness. If an encyclopedia's success can be measured by the quantity of its content, then Wikipedia is a standout. In its short lifetime, its scope has extended beyond that of the traditional stalwarts. At the time of writing, it consisted of 300 000 articles and 90 million words and was continually growing. By contrast *Britannica* has 85 000 articles and 55 million words.

All of sudden, the encyclopedic ideal of permanence has been cast aside, in a tacit acknowledgment that knowledge has always been changing; and that only the rigours of traditional publishing have held the pace of change in check. The internet, with Wikipedia, has succeeded in making another invisible visible. Only this time, the invisibility has also flattened the steps in the evolving body of knowledge. Rather than platforms every few metres (as one might picture the traditional print encyclopedia), Wikipedia is a long, incline. A ramp which climbs incessantly to an undefined destination. As the cliché goes, it demonstrates that the journey is the important thing.

Of course, there are those who argue that the ramp is actually going down, not up, plunging at a rapidly accelerating rate. For these people, it is quality that counts, not quantity. And Wikipedia entries can be uneven. Even its publishers acknowledge the difficulties involved in ensuring that articles meet appropriate standards of research and writing. However, it is not a problem unique to the Wikipedia experience. A recent study by the journal *Nature* compared the publishing models of Wikipedia and *Britannica*, and concluded that the 'difference in accuracy was not particularly great'. What's more, errors were corrected far more rapidly in Wikipedia. One researcher suggested that:

> People will find it shocking to see how many errors there are in *Britannica* … Print encyclopedias are often set up as the gold standard of information quality against which the failings of faster or cheaper resources can be compared. These findings remind us that we have an 18-carat standard, not a 24-carat one.[16]

The *Nature* article provoked a furious response from *Britannica*, and it's clear that the argument is far from over.

Rather, the debate merely reflects the tensions involved in a cultural shift from one of deferring to the experts *without*, to embracing the experts *within*. It is as monumental as the shift from blindly obeying the spoken word of church and monarch to being able to read and write books that propose alternative views. Wikipedia is a dynamic book, if you like, which relegates the permanence of the printed page to the metaphorical dustbin.

▶▶ Not all that glitters

There are, of course, issues with the blog/wiki models of reading and writing. From an author's point of view, there are issues of recompense. Writing a blog is not yet an effective way to make a decent living. (I'm talking mortgage, kids and the occasional trip to a deserted Pacific Island to unwind.) Using Google AdSense, and blogging about their favourite shareware, a computer science major might be able to earn beer money. But not too many are quitting their day jobs just yet. And it's also problematic for that other form of recompense; credibility, both socially and professionally. Whilst blogs are now a kind of cultural calling card for anybody with a mouse and an internet connection, they remain the domain of the wired. If there is such a thing as mainstream, the blog is not yet it. More importantly, for academics, journalists and others who write for a living, the blog is yet to gain required professional status. A blog will not yet get you tenure. Or a Pulitzer. (Although I do have to add the caveat of 'yet'.)

From the reader's point of view, other issues may surface. Print culture has fixity embedded. The new online reading and writing culture doesn't. It is, by its very nature *dynamic*. The great advantage of the online realm is also its great disadvantage. Last week's wiki entry on Fiji might be different this week. My blog is not guaranteed to present a consistent point of view. To the writer, this might be an advantage, but the reader needs to reconfigure their idea of reading; reshape their cultural expectations and incorporate the dimension of time in their citations (subconscious or otherwise). In other words, rather than saying that 'Sherman Young reckons that the book is dead', the new culture demands that the reader understand 'In 2007,

Sherman Young reckoned that the book was dead.'

But most of all, there is the sense that the new media audience *reads differently*. Ideas of expertise have been replaced by notions of engagement. No longer do readers rely on their source to be absolutely authoritative. Instead, they themselves expect to double-check and cross-reference; to ensure that the material they are reading is accurate and appropriate. Today, we are encountering investigative readers, what media theorist, David Marshall calls 'readers as researchers'.[17] It's harder. But it's also a more accurate reflection of reality which was once disguised by the apparent permanence of the printed book and the (so-called) expertise contained within those books.

▶▶| Whither publishing?

The new online media forms demonstrate more than just the blurring of production and consumption. What they clearly demonstrate is a blurring between writing and publishing. Websites made it easy. Blogs make it doubly so. Wikis transcend the argument. Some argue that *writing is now publishing*. But I don't think that's entirely accurate. Publishing blogs and websites is useful, valuable and a terrific way of communicating and sharing ideas. But blogs and websites are generally not *publications* in the way books are. I prefer to think of them as *public writing*.

Public writing is different from book publishing. Not better or worse, but different. It has attributes that books do not: a quick response time, immediate communication, an easier entry path into human conversation. But books and public writing should co-exist because books do something different. They are the more reflective and contemplative parts of that conversation, and all the more essential for their slower pace.

As we saw in Chapter 2, book culture depends on authority and *authors* are the source of that authority. The very act of writing several tens of thousands of words on a particular topic demands that authors know their subject more deeply than most would. A good book requires that an author be well read in the topic; that he has understood the question and the possible answers; that he has mounted an argument and managed to communicate it convincingly.

For the most part, authority is conferred because writing a book (for most people) is hard. It takes a long time. It is a slow process. Whatever the genre, the journey of writing a book is not an easy one. Fictional accounts demand acts of the imagination and somersaults of plot that are generally not dreamed up overnight. Genuine characterisations need thought. Ideas need to be considered in detail and reflected upon. Non-fiction titles make different demands. Facts need to be checked. Ideas need to be made convincing. Rhetoric needs to be balanced with something resembling evidence: anecdotes and examples to illustrate each point; statistics to satisfy the more rigorous reader. So writing a book is a challenge, which is as it should be. The process of writing (or more to the point, of reading, thinking and writing) is the journey that must be made to reach the destination. Authority does not come from merely having an idea. Authority, in book culture, is bestowed on someone because they have *authored* something.

Part of the authoring process is its gentle pace. It takes time to properly write something; and one of the most valuable things about book culture is that writing a book forces the author to slow down. That pace is not simply because writing a book is a big project. Writing a piece of computer software is an equally big project. But writing software, whilst sharing similar patterns of thought, reflection and refinement has a further imposition of functionality. It has to work on a computer. So, the pace of that creative act is dictated by a further constraint, and the slowness that writing a book demands is not possible in the software realm. Books are creative acts whose only constraints are imposed by the author. As such, they are a retreat to the slow; to the thoughtful and reflective in an otherwise frenetic world.

What's more, the long hours spent massaging an author's raw text into a form acceptable to the reading public; the editor's skill in drawing out the core ideas and shaping them into books is largely missing in the blogosphere. The problem however, is that it is largely missing in book publishing too.

Where the new media excels is in creating alternative possibilities for validation – open and transparent avenues that provide a place where writers and readers can connect – without the dead weight of a publisher getting in the way. But so far, only the publishing process turns writers into authors, and ideas into books. However, new media technologies have blurred the lines between writing and publishing. Whilst those steeped in book culture might clearly see the difference, others couldn't care less and are busy adapting their writing and reading to new concepts of production and consumption. The challenge for book publishers remains. Public writing means that communicating with words is no longer the sole domain of people with printing presses. Processes of validation are no longer in the hands of people with warehouses packed with printed books. But books are essential to the human conversation, book culture makes a vital contribution. It is up to publishers to properly define and defend the book, and its culture.

▶▶| CHAPTER 5.
What do publishers do?

America's media and entertainment industry has a gross (as it were) revenue of $316.8 billion a year. If we subtract the income derived from worthy journalism and the publishing of serious books, that leaves $316.8 billion.

PJ O'Rourke[1]

In their introduction to *The Future of the Book in the Digital Age*,[2] Angus Phillips and Bill Cope summarise the 'complaints heard all the way up and down the book production supply chain'. At the production end, it is becoming more difficult for authors to be published; and when published, authors feel that they don't get the attention (and royalties) that they deserve from their publishers. As the market becomes more competitive publishers see their margins decreasing. As a result, the smaller ones are finding it more difficult to survive and many are closing down or being absorbed into larger conglomerates. As well, many tasks that used to be core to book publishing (such as editing and design) are outsourced in a frantic attempt to reduce costs. Then, the companies that print the books are subject to global competition, with titles increasingly being printed in countries with lower production costs. Once printed and shipped across the planet, retailers are not immune. Bookstores struggle to find a balance between keeping *enough* stock and the *right* stock in a retail environment in which books now compete with a plethora of multimedia entertainment products. Add the distractions of newer non-traditional sources for books such as discount stores and online bookstores, and the old-fashioned bookshop is struggling. Meanwhile, the rest of us, the readers, whinge about the high price of books, and the lack of selection and availability in their local bookshop. Thanks to the internet and the joys of the world wide web and peer-to-peer filesharing, we've become used to instant gratification at zero cost.

The technology of the book is struggling, with writers, readers and publishers all trying to come to terms with a brave new world. All is not as it was, and readers and writers are responding in the only way they know how: by deserting the sinking ship. As we have seen, readers are rapidly finding other forms of entertainment and sources of information; writers are discovering new outlets for their creativity and validation for their output.

Which leaves the industry to figure out a way forward. Book publishers are under pressure at both ends. There are consumer demands for cheaper and more instantly gratifying reading material. And there are the real demands of business. Like it or not, despite the duality of publishing and the tradition of balancing art and economics, the art cannot exist if there is no business. In an era where short-term market-driven decisions are de rigueur, the balance has shifted; business has become the priority. Creating a book culture is no longer central to what book publishers do. Instead, readers and writers look elsewhere for their intellectual and cultural gratification. Tied to the object of the book, many publishers have relinquished their role. For them, the book is already dead, replaced by the need to ship objects of the same name.

▶▶◀ That was then

The book industry is a strange beast. It bathes in the warm romantic glow of an imagined history; one firmly based on notions of literature, high culture and ideas. The book, in its leather-bound glory was a touchstone for everything that the world should be, and the people who created these icons considered publishing to be different from other industries. According to those who were there at the time, in the good old days, publishers knew that one day the books would come good; that the world would recognise the worth of the talent they were shaping. They were not driven by instantaneous sales figures, but by the judgment of time passing.

Figures such as Jason Epstein and André Schiffrin romanticise their early years in the publishing industry. Epstein founded Anchor Books and was the editorial director of Random House. In *Book Business,* he catalogues a shift in the industry for the worse. In *The Business of Books,* Schiffrin, former publisher at Pantheon Books is equally adamant and negative. They remember when publishing was as much about ideas as business; a cottage industry in which people cared and literature mattered. Books were seen as something that could change the world. To Epstein, the project was modernism and the book was how it would be achieved.[3] To Schiffrin, their duty was to make a profit by nurturing the best writing, and supporting books that publishers judged worthwhile: 'Even some of the mass-market publishing houses were trying to broaden the boundaries, to seek new readers, and to raise general levels of literacy and knowledge.'[4]

Then, publishers were like family for their authors. Their often humble offices became a 'second home'[5] for writers, a place where they could hang out and be welcomed at any time of the night or day. The author was central to the publisher's existence and success; a success that was not measured in revenues, but in reviews. And in the social and cultural impact of the book. The need for profits every fiscal quarter was less important than allowing sufficient time for books and authors to have an impact. That commitment was inherent in what book publishers did, what book culture was about.

Authors and their books needed time to resonate with the literary public. Moreover they needed support right down the line. Not only editors and publishers, but sales representatives and booksellers had to understand the value of each book, appreciate its worth and inform an appropriate market of that worth. As the author's literary merits grew, the payback would come; the growing value of their backlist would more than compensate for years of patronage: 'it was understood that entire categories of books, particularly new fiction and poetry, were bound to lose money. It was assumed that believing in authors was an investment for the future ...'[6]

In that mythical golden age, *book culture* mattered; ideas were as important as money and publishers struggled to find that balance between art and business. It was the role of the publishing house to sort the worthy from the unworthy, to decide what was important in the culture of the time. The book was an essential component of humanity's project, and publishers were key players in disseminating ideas and kick-starting the human conversation. This required faith, and massive self-belief, a genuine sense that publishing was a noble calling. Publishers were on a mission, if not *from* God, then *to be* God.

▶▶ This is now

Today's publishers still see themselves as the arbiters of what should and shouldn't be read in print, but it is hard to imagine that the modern multinational book publisher has the same flexibility, nor the same desire to find that delicate balance between culture and commerce. In the latter part of the twentieth century, media ownership became more concentrated and book publishers succumbed to that business maxim of grow or die. Smaller publishers were devoured by bigger ones, purchased for their (now profitable) backlists or the prestige of their imprint; bigger publishers were in turn gobbled up by the mega corporations, many of whom saw book publishing as just another arm of their multimedia empires.

Schiffrin describes the demise of the imprint he ran at Random House in the late 1980s. Always an adventurous publisher of interesting titles, Pantheon's literary ideas were somewhat out of place at the behemoth publishing house. The imprint contributed titles as varied as the *For Beginners* series, Art Spiegelman's *Maus*, Anita Brookner's novels, new translations of Franz Kafka and Günter Grass's Nobel Prize winning *The Tin Drum*. Things came to a head when Alberto Vitale was installed as the new boss of Random House in 1989. Whilst introduced as 'a man of culture and sensitivity', it was clear that Vitale was a businessman first and foremost. This was made apparent by his 'admission that he was far too busy to read a book ... not a book could be seen on his shelves; the photographs on display were not of authors but of his yacht'.[7]

After a bloody and public dispute over what to publish, Schiffrin was disposed and Pantheon was reinvented. The new publisher changed its publishing philosophy, steering the imprint away from political works until it was unrecognisable. Books that questioned social and cultural mores and the more demanding intellectual titles were abandoned. From being an important publisher of social critique, Pantheon's list of lead titles came to include a collection of Barbie doll photographs.[8] The Pantheon experience was not unique. Larger corporations brought in management who established a new order. The intellectual and cultural standards of the past were no longer to be tolerated: 'They were there to make money and for no other reason.'[9]

After decades of merger and acquisition, economic rationalisation and shareholder driven change, the mainstream publishing industry is dominated by a small number of players. Bertelsmann, Holtzbrinck and Hachette in Europe, Pearson in the UK and News Corp and Viacom in the USA essentially control the industry.

HarperCollins emerged from News Limited's 1987 acquisition of Harper & Row in the USA and its 1989 purchase of the UK publisher Collins. Once a bastion of the literary world, the 'new'

HarperCollins focused on commercial titles and tie-ins to its other entertainment properties. Where the Harper's list might have contained such interesting titles as Robert Heilbroner's *The Future as History*,[10] recent prominent titles are less convincing. According to its own publicity, HarperCollins's 'publishing sensation of 2003' was a book about a celebrity footballer, David Beckham's *My Side*.[11]

Simon & Schuster may have begun as a crossword publisher with an entrepreneurial streak[12] but it evolved into a publisher with a string of prize winning literary authors and a diverse backlist. As it grew larger, eventually to become part of the Viacom corporation (since split into Viacom and CBS Corporation), it too saw a shift. Michael Korda was Simon & Schuster's chief editor for many years. He pursued highly commercial bestsellers exemplified by Harold Robbins and Jacqueline Sussan and during his tenure, was certain that 'celebrity books are the titles that will make or break firms'.[13] Korda was probably correct. Book publishers have thrived on commercial movie tie-ins and celebrity books. Whilst some resisted, the industry moved on without them. In a battle for profitability, the dilution of book culture was the price that had to be paid.

To the multimedia multinationals, books are just one of many cross-media opportunities that can be exploited in sophisticated sales and marketing campaigns. A successful book is one that sells millions and generates cross-pollination possibilities. So, *Harry Potter* hardbacks and paperbacks (with different covers to appeal to different target audiences) become the *Harry Potter* movie franchise, the PlayStation gaming series, and the coffee cup, lunchbox and soft toy experience. The book, whilst the origin of the *Harry Potter* species, is but one part of the empire. Many of the last decade's bestsellers have been movie tie-ins, and it is often the case that 'the most successful books enjoy four incarnations: hardcover, paperback, movie and video/DVD'.[14] The chain works the other way as well. Just as movies have emerged from books, books have emerged from movies (*Star Wars*) and videogames (*Halo* and *Myst*). And it's not unusual for a title to come full circle. For example, Ian Fleming's *James Bond* novels sparked a number of films which borrowed little from the original stories. *Casino Royale* is just the latest in a long line of movies whose only resemblance to the original novel is in the spelling of the title. In fact, the 1979 film *Moonraker* was so dissimilar to Fleming's 1955 book that the screen version was novelised by Christopher Wood and published by Cape as a different *Moonraker* novel. This is the new reality. A book version of *Finding Nemo* is guaranteed to shift far more copies than a new novel by an unknown writer; for publishers the financially responsible choice is obvious.

Epstein and Schiffrin suggest that in the 'golden age', there was no need for such a choice; publishers were able to cross-subsidise their less profitable ventures. Today, the suits would argue that typical margins no longer support that kind of luxury. Booklovers might think that books deserve special treatment. But in a large corporation, they are just another commodity that has to be produced, distributed and sold. On the balance sheet, they are no different from whatever else that corporation makes, whether they are shower curtains or videotapes. So the numbers generated by the book part of the trade are expected to match the margins made by other divisions within the corporate empire. Historically, book margins have been around 10–12 per cent, as compared to 20 per cent for other entertainment sectors.[15] In the quest to match the required returns, it's little surprise that the apparent indulgences of the past have been cast aside. Instead of publishing decisions being editorial decisions, they are now marketing ones; understandable in the newly competitive environment.

Unfortunately, those apparent indulgences are exactly the things that created a book culture. Whilst considered indulgences by the bean counters, they represent the key ingredients that *make books books.* (Accountants might argue here that the cost of book culture is the equivalent of a 10 per cent margin.) Much of that margin is protected by making marketable publishing decisions. No longer are the larger publishers willing to take a risk on unknown or marginal authors. No longer does an author's writing or ideas matter as much as their potential sales. Instead publishers search for safety, books which will almost certainly reach an appropriate and profitable target.

VS Naipaul won the 1971 Booker Prize for his novel *Free State*. It was widely praised at the time, and Naipaul is a member of the late twentieth century literary canon. His books may not attract the attention of the latest and newest authors, but as a Booker winner, his presence in the backlist is assured. In late 2005, the *Sunday Times* sent the opening chapters of *Free State* to 20 publishers and literary agents, changing its title and the name of the author. Not one of the recipients of those chapters considered them worthy of publication.[16] In 2006, the *Australian* conducted a similar experiment, sending Chapter 3 of Patrick White's *The Eye of the Storm* under a pseudonym to 12 publishers and agents. Again, the novel was rejected by all.[17] White, of course, won the Nobel Prize in Literature in 1973, and is one of Australia's key literary figures. Today, it appears that both award-winning novelists would not be published except for the fact that they *have been published*.

In defence of the decision not to publish the White novel, Shona Martyn (HarperCollins's Australian publishing director) suggested that the editors 'may have recognised the literary talent but made the decision it was not viable'. Literary agent Lyn Tranter was more direct. She called the experiment 'piss weak' because White is no longer read generally, and doesn't sell today. 'I am looking at one thing and one thing only: can I sell it? And the answer is no, I can't sell *The Eye of the Storm*.' Martyn concurred: 'publishing is a business and we are looking at what Australian readers want to buy. If more people wanted to read more books instead of watching celebrity ice-skating, I would be delighted.' Matthew Kelly, publisher with Hachette in Australia argues 'People who want more literary fiction published too easily ignore one crucial question: Why should publishers produce books that do not pay their way?'[18]

So the brutal new reality is that it is no longer viable to publish Nobel Prize-winning writing. At a time when publishers are more risk-averse than ever, aspiring authors need to find a different approach. Great writing is not enough.

In Australia, the financial pressures of being a book publisher just don't seem to add up to a viable business with several shutting up shop in recent years. As a result, there has been much hand-wringing about the state of Australian writing. Celebrated, and widely-published writers like award winning novelist Brian Castro have suffered the fate of the rejection slip. His sales weren't sufficient to create enough interest from the larger publishing companies. (Castro was picked up by the independent Giramondo. Not all established writers manage to land in that safety net.)

Whether publishers have a responsibility towards the telling of indigenous narratives is an intriguing question. In a market-driven economy, where everything is about the bottom line, patriotic notions seem quaint. But like public-service broadcasting, whose cultural value cannot be measured in dollars, a book publisher's role has historically been more than that of a typical media business. Books, argue booklovers, are important cultural documents and a key component in any nation-building narrative. Maybe. But book publishers are *businesses*. Most of them are multinational, and do not suffer under any sense of patriotic obligation. As Carmen Lawrence noted, major publishers 'feel no obligation to add to the canon of Australian literature'.[19] Merchant bankers are not required to prop up national economies in a competitive global marketplace, nor do car manufacturers, airlines or clothing firms labour under any more than a notional national interest. A book culture might desire such an approach but publishers are now required to play by a different set of rules. They are market-driven. Editors and publishers are profit centres and must post appropriate results for each title; supporting an author whose books have not done well in the past is no longer an option.

Indeed major publishers probably feel less obliged to support the indigenous product because direct government support for literature (as opposed to the shoe industry) does still exist. In this country, the Australia Council funds writers' centres and writers themselves. However, it's clear that this division between state-funded and market-driven works has not really increased the readership of Australian literature.

As margins are forced lower, publishers are sticking with established sellers or only going for newcomers with that something extra, like celebrity. Hence, the rise of both the celebrity autobiography and the celebrity novel. In Australia, Tara Moss trades on her fame as an ex-model and society A-lister to become a published crime novelist, and in the UK, Katie Price, the model known as Jordan, has a two novel deal with Random House. It's easier to sell books that have been written by celebrities; they are already well known, can generate their own publicity and their books have immediate appeal to the public. Both Jordan and Moss may be fine writers, but there are many fine writers who have not received a publishing deal.

As well as bowing to higher profit margins, part of the pressure comes from the increasing accountability required by the trade. In Epstein's day, publishers could justify an author's continued publication by citing somewhat rubbery sales figures and pointing to media attention in a few prominent journals. Today, book sales are meticulously tracked and the use of data generated by systems such as Bookscan has brought a far more reliable picture of what is selling and what is not. Publishers can jump on that data and decide empirically that a book is not worth publishing, because the author's previous book did not do the business. Today, the second novel is unlikely to be published if the first does not work.

Short-term goals can, however, skew things. The goose may be slaughtered before sufficient time has been devoted to its fattening. Not supporting an author with low sales prevents her from developing a readership (and authorship) over time and possibly becoming more influential with her third, fourth or fifth book. Instant sales data also tends to emphasise the bestsellers; sales success breeds more attention. Bookshops will track trends rather than satisfy their own gut instinct and publishers will highlight those titles with the good numbers. So backlists suffer; bookshops are more likely to purchase more of a currently hyped title than stock a copy or two of a backlist title that may or may not sell. And whilst this might be good for business, it is bad for books.

It's easy to be cynical about today's book trade. The bestseller lists are dominated by marketing-driven titles; those anti-books whose success is dependent not on readers, but buyers. And whose creation relies not on authors, but writers. An anti-book need not be a blockbuster; although it is undoubtedly sales driven, rather than ideas driven. As such, its success depends on an appropriate marketing spin. On publishing, as suggested previously, a *hook*, not a *book*. It's a vicious circle. The more publishers try to succeed in the new mediascape, the more they turn to anti-books, forcing more readers elsewhere. Which in turn drives publishers to more market-driven approaches. But I think that we can break the cycle. Books *can* be ideas driven, and the new technologies can provide a tool for that to happen. But more on that in a later chapter.

The current fad in sales-driven approaches is known as 'specialty-marketing' and involves creating books for sale in 'alternative outlets'. For example, do it yourself books are sold in hardware stores across the United States, and cookbooks in cookware outlets and delis. Some publishers create books tailored to non-traditional sales outlets. Penguin produced a special issue of its *Secret Recipes* cookbook and sold 100 000 copies on a cable television shopping channel. HarperCollins reprinted the cover of its *Fondue* books to match the decor of the Urban Outfitters clothing chain.[20] For many publishers, specialty-marketing is the fastest growing part of their retail strategy; in the last four years, Simon & Schuster's sales in that area have grown by 50 per cent, and are now larger than total sales to independent bookstores.[21]

There is, of course, nothing wrong with producing such book-objects, except when the task is done *instead of producing real books*. A focus entirely on these sales means that there is less emphasis on other, less prominent titles; the so-called midlist. American data suggests that smaller titles; those with print runs of a few thousand are no longer being printed by the larger conglomerates. While some *do* still publish such titles, books with smaller print runs do not get the support they require.[22] The warning bells were being sounded as long ago as 1947, when Frank Mott wrote:

> there is a real danger to proper book publishing in the emphasis on mass distribution. Only a small proportion of new books are potential bestsellers. The thousands of valuable works that ought to be published but which cannot be depended upon for more than a very modest return on investment must not be forgotten in the scramble for mass markets.[23]

Gayle Feldman argues that over the last half century, 'the distortions in the business have become more extreme'.[24] Publishers no longer devote resources to books unless they are considered sure things. Authors who are lucky enough to get a publishing contract often find that there is no money for editorial guidance. Midlist books (those with US print runs of 5000 to 15 000 copies and of a similar scale relative to the bestsellers elsewhere) do not have the budget for the required level of support. Instead, the editing role of the publisher is largely delegated to the author. Left to their own devices, they do the best they can, pay for their own independent editorial assistance, or suffer the critics' barbs.

The *Columbia Journalism Review* highlighted the example of Stacy Sullivan.[25] Having secured a contract for a book on the war in Kosovo, she was expecting a reasonable amount of editorial feedback and assistance. Instead, almost none was forthcoming: 'I had turned in what I thought was a draft and I had gotten back this copyedited manuscript,' Sullivan says. 'They were just going to print that. And it was so rough. There was no way.' But the book was already on the conveyor belt. It was listed in the next season's catalogue and the sales representatives had begun pitching it to booksellers. Everyone, including her agent, told her there was really nothing to be done. She then edited it herself, cutting out about 300 pages.

The same holds true of marketing and publicity. Publishers commonly do next to no publicity or marketing for most midlist titles. They are unlikely to be highlighted by sales reps, and will not be part of the (expensive) co-operative marketing material with bookshops. David Kirkpatrick, in a report for the Authors Guild in America, suggests that 'midlist books wind up being printed but not really published'. He paints a picture of how a typical midlist title might have to compete for attention, even within the publisher itself:

> Even high-ranking editors sometimes have less than a minute in front of a crowd at a seasonal conference to pitch a title's merits to their house's sales staff. The titles on each list are competing for a finite quantity of attention and money. Publishers and editors have an incentive to put their clout behind the titles with the strongest commercial prospects. Simon & Schuster, for example, introduced no other new titles the month it published Stephen King's latest novel.[26]

More than likely, the author will be required to pay for her own book launch. Instead of actual *marketing*, publicity is 'review driven'. Rather than arrange readings and signings, organise interviews or aggressively pursue reviews, the publisher might send out a few galleys to the national media in the hope of a response. As with the editing, the author is once again on her own. For many authors, publishers just *print and ship*.

▶▶ Behind the retail facade

Walking into a large suburban bookstore makes a liar out of me. It *is* possible to find books that are not blockbusters or Hollywood tie-ins or celebrity cosmetic surgery hints or how-to-guides for the newly wealthy. For every book that sits in a display stand surrounded by expensive point of sale material, there is one that sits on a corner shelf under the title Art History. For every crime novel written by an ex-model, there's one by a Booker Prize shortlister. Despite the rantings of people like me (and Epstein and Schiffrin), there are a lot of books on the shelves.

Real life is not black and white but is instead textured shades of grey; it's not a zero-sum game. There *are* still lots of books in the bookshops; but there are also lots of books that *should* be in the bookshops, but aren't. Publishers might be publishing some interesting titles, but there are many more that they are not publishing. The fact is that their ability to publish those interesting titles has diminished because, for the most part they are not permitted to cross-subsidise. Instead, each book has to exist on its own merits.

What's more, the task of nurturing new writers has been left to independent publishers. But those publishers are disappearing. From around 200 'significant' publishers in literary London in the 1950s, there are now fewer than 30. Even some hold-outs such as Fourth Estate have recently been subsumed into the multinational giants.[27] Publishing unproven authors can be risky and the returns are often marginal.

Let's look at some numbers. It's a little hard to be definitive because every book in every country is different. What's more, publishers can be quite protective of their actual economic performance, but the following are *indicative* figures from book industry insiders.

The first is an Australian publication, a typical 'small' book like this one. Fixed production costs (covering editing and proofing, design and the like) are around $6500. Print costs for 3000 copies run to $7500, which means that those copies cost $14000 to produce. Given a recommended retail price of $29.95 and an average shop discount of 42.5 per cent, the publisher would receive $15.66 per copy sold (after sales tax is accounted for). The cost of sales and distribution works out at about $5.95 a copy and a typical author's royalty would be 10 per cent of net sales, or $1.56 a copy, leaving $8.15 earnings per copy. So the summary is:

Table 5.1: Fixed costs for 3000 copies

item	cost
fixed design and production	$6500
printing	$7500
total fixed costs	**$14000**

Table 5.2: Earnings per copy

item	amount per copy
recommended retail price	$29.95
GST	$2.72
bookshop discount	$11.57
publisher receives	**$15.66**
cost of sales/distribution (38%)	$5.95
author royalty (10%)	$1.56
total costs	**$7.51**
earnings per book sold	**$8.15**

Table 5.3: Potential profit after deducting fixed costs

books sold	earnings at $8.15	less fixed costs	profit
3 000	$24 450	$14 000	$10 450
2 000	$16 300	$14 000	$2 300
1 000	$8 150	$14 000	-$5 850

The 'profit' for each title has to cover the publishers' overheads, which includes staff salaries, rents, warehousing stock and all of those other little things that make up a business. And don't forget that a book is not really sold until the bookseller sells it to a paying customer and then actually pays the publisher. Most publishers operate on a sale and return policy which allows booksellers to return (for credit) unsold titles within a certain period of time.

A slightly larger US example confirms the precarious economics of book publishing.[28] This title is a typical mass market paperback with a print run of 35 000 copies. Editing costs are $1405. Artwork, design and typesetting costs are $8900. Printing and distribution for 35 000 copies come to $19 925. The marketing budget is $6400. The total cost is about $36 000. The summary is:

Table 5.4: Fixed costs for 35 000 copies

item	cost
editorial	$1 405
fixed design and production	$8 900
printing and distribution	$19 925
marketing	$6 000
total fixed costs	**$36 230**

Table 5.5: Earnings per copy

item	cost per copy
recommended retail price	$6.99
bookshop discount (average per book)	$2.80
author royalty (fixed per book)	$0.56
earnings per book sold	**$3.63**

Table 5.6: Potential profit after deducting fixed costs

books sold	earnings	profit
30 000	$108 900	$72 670
20 000	$72 600	$36 370
10 000	$36 300	$70

Again, the 'profit' has to take into account overheads, returns and (in this example) the cost of sales. And while projected sales figures might look appealing, each title is a gamble; the average mass market paperback sells one in three copies printed.

It's easy to see that publishing individual books is risky and can lead to financial loss. Publishers pursue blockbusters and market-driven publishing projects for good reasons. Economies of scale kick in, reducing printing costs and lowering the per-copy amount spent on fixed costs. A focused marketing spend can reduce the risk and if successful, large profits are possible. It's not unusual for half a publisher's overhead costs to be taken care of by the sales of its bestselling author.[29]

The larger publishers are public companies and have legal obligations to their shareholders. They also have obligations to their other stakeholders: employees, suppliers, even their authors and readers. No matter how much one might want to re-live a nostalgic past, the good old days existed within an entirely different economic context. Today, business is business. Lose money publishing books, and there won't be much more publishing to come.

▶▶ Rest in peace

In short, the golden age is gone for good and won't be back. Whilst it's nice to reminisce about the good old days of publishing, it's impossible to imagine a modern day publishing company, working within contemporary market constraints, again prioritising the ideals of a book culture. Too much has changed, and there's simply no going back.

But the book trade is still different. Some publishers do care about books and ideas and are passionate about creating a book culture that matters. People attracted to publishing want to trade in ideas, not kitchenware; they are enamoured of the myth of publishing and want to be part of changing the world. Even in modern day publishing houses we can still see reflections of the golden age. The cynical multimedia synergies that dot the wider mediascape have not yet fully infiltrated the book world. For example, you don't often see television ads for paperback novels in the middle of *Desperate Housewives*. Nor do you see ads for *Desperate Housewives* in the pages of paperback novels. The fact that so many books are still published, despite the financial risks involved, suggests that a book culture continues to exist. Not everything is pulped. Publishers maintain a backlist of sorts and store palettes of unsold books in vast warehouses in the hope that they might sell. And the sales and marketing of books is not the hard-sell of other media industries. Selling books is more about publicity, generating word of mouth, promoting authors and leveraging literary events such as writers' festivals.

For all of that, book culture is no longer central to the book business. The need to produce and shift objects and make money doing so has distracted even the most devoted. Peter Dimock, a former editor at Random House in the United States suggests that publishing books has become about selling an object that encapsulates the entire book experience. The object is more important than its contents. And the design of those objects and their packaging has come to dominate the production process. The book itself has ceased to matter:

> We were subliminally promising the buyer, through our packaging and accompanying synoptic copy, that no difficult intellectual effort would be required. We were promising that the sensation and the effect of intellectual and aesthetic engagement – the value of having read the book (slowly, deeply, richly, challengingly, threateningly) – were available by merely buying it.[30]

Constrained by economics, the object is the focus. Everything else that is valuable about books is relegated to a distant last place. And it's easy to see why. Notwithstanding the individual budgetary examples previously cited, the cost of publishing is largely the cost of producing and moving objects. Australian data shows that in 2003–04, book publishers spent $316 million on printing, $202 million on importing books and $94 million on distribution. By comparison, line item expenditure for authors was $77 million and a mere $45 million for editorial and publishing fees and salaries.[31]

▶▎   Bring out the dead

So there's an obvious way to make book culture viable in the new economy. By getting out of the printing business, the business of books can be reinvigorated. Imagine removing the printing and distribution costs from the production budget of a typical book. Then take away some of the artwork costs. All of a sudden the expenditure side of the equation is much, much smaller. *Then* remove the risk of returns, and the warehousing costs. Rethink the marketing to take advantage of newer publicity mechanisms and information filters. By killing the physical object of the book, you breathe new life into the book itself.

The book publishing industry shares a branding problem with other media outlets. Its brands are its authors, not its corporate structures or imprints, only a handful of which have recognition value outside of industry functions. Just as nobody remembers who publishes the music of the *Rolling Stones*, most people couldn't tell you who publishes William Faulkner or Dan Brown. Instead of a handful of brands (such as Coke and Diet Coke), book publishers need to develop as many brands as they have authors, which nobody has the resources to do properly. Aside from the blockbusters, selling books is about niches and matching the right book to the right reader. The small bookshop fails in this task because it can't hold the stock. The big superstore fails because it is simply an overwhelming experience; and even the megamarts are constrained by the sheer physicality of the printed form. By necessity, publishers need to focus their marketing efforts (their points of sale, dumpbins, catalogues and table displays) on a select few titles that will do well.

An obvious first step is to eliminate that initial guesswork of how many copies of a particular title to print. So-called print-on-demand (POD) technology allows publishers to do just that: print copies only when they are bought. Some publishers are experimenting with POD for short print runs, but the economies are not particularly attractive. Per unit cost for anything but very small quantities is higher than traditional printing.

The next step might be to localise the technology and use it instead for one-off print runs. Instead of shelves of seldom-sold titles, Jason Epstein envisages a series of POD kiosks which allow book buyers to browse the backlist and generate a printed copy immediately; in much the same way that some music stores allow purchasers to compile collections of music and burn CDs on demand. The idea of an instant book, culled from a vast archive of titles is definitely appealing, and has the potential to eliminate stock holding limitations.

A different type of POD service eliminates the publisher; allowing what the pundits call disintermediation or the skipping of the middleman. If writing is now publishing, then why bother with publishers? Lulu.com does away with that infrastructure, and allows individuals to publish real, printed books and sell them. Lulu users upload their book's contents, and either choose a cover design or create their own, set a price and the book is made available on the Lulu website. A purchaser clicks to buy (perhaps after reading an online sample) and the Lulu infrastructure creates a book object and delivers it as requested. I've bought a couple of books from Lulu and they are physically indistinguishable from ones I've bought in bookshops. And the book's contents are no worse than many 'properly' published titles, although the lack of a publisher means that potential readers (and writers) might need to exercise more (or perhaps a different type of) rigour when selecting their purchases.

But Lulu does not really compete with traditional book publishing. It provides a mechanical service that appeals to readers comfortable with newer forms of reputation management. What it illustrates is an experiment in reconfiguring the production and distribution of the print object that might be a useful model for others.

If book publishers no longer print, are they still necessary? The answer is 'yes'. The validation of writers allowed by the new media technologies is different from the role played by publishers. Blog popularity rankings, wiki collaborations, reputation managers and the like are extremely useful tools and valuable contributions to humanity's project. But the book still has its place; where more reflective and considered ideas and the conversation around them are discussed. And an integral part of the technology of books is *publishing*; a process which creates books from texts, and turns writers into authors.

The new modes of public writing discussed in the previous chapter might be a useful form of communication, but such self-publishing does not replace the work of a publisher. Even if all they do is slow down the pace of publication, then that is enough. A dispassionate editor does more than just slow things down; she inserts distance into the text, so that its usefulness can be tested before it is published. And that extra time and distance is what makes a book a book.

But to save itself, book culture needs to discard the object. By tying itself to print on paper, the book is restricted to playing in the game of scarcity economics. The need to produce, distribute, store and return printed books means that the current incarnation of the publishing industry is probably as good as it gets. In the context of fiscal responsibility and shareholder return, book culture can have no voice. The real craft of book-making – publishing, editing, designing words – has largely been lost in the need to manage the cost of shipping objects.

The new technologies afford us opportunities to play in a different type of economy – what some call an economy of abundance – where the high costs of keeping physical objects is replaced with the much lower cost of maintaining digital ones. Given that books are about ideas, stepping into the virtual economy seems logical. The object simply gets in the way. And yet, so many seem to confuse the object with the book itself.

⏭ CHAPTER 6.
Objects of desire

People want to own physical books because of their visceral appeal (often this is accompanied by a little sermonette on how good books smell, or how good they look on a bookshelf, or how evocative an old curry stain in the margin can be) ...

Cory Doctorow[1]

People who love things are often confused about what exactly it is they love. Car lovers for example. Some revheads love the cars themselves; the richer ones have garages full of beautiful exotic machinery capable of insane speeds at which they're never driven. These enthusiasts spend their Sundays blissfully turtle-waxing Lamborghinis. Others love what the car makes possible; the apparent freedom to go wherever whenever, or the sheer adrenalin rush of travelling as fast as possible; the visceral experience of speed. Many carlovers embrace both aspects. But if pushed to choose, most would probably admit that the object without the velocity; the sculpture without the speed is less than satisfying. Whilst a Ferrari Enzo might be a beautiful thing, part of its beauty is how it drives.

Booklovers are the same. Some love the objects themselves. They are attracted to musty leather bound volumes, gasp at original editions and swoon at impressive typography on heavy acid-free paper. Others care more about the words; the stories and ideas within the book are worth more than the containers in which they reside. Many booklovers are fans of both the object and its contents; whilst the text is key, the object is still important. At the very least, it tells the world who he is, like a well-cut suit.

To some, being seen with *Life a User's Manual* (or at least having it lying on the coffee table) is as important as actually reading it. A recent survey of 2100 people in the UK found that one in three had bought books 'solely to look intelligent'.[2]

Booklovers defend the book as if the object and its contents are inseparable; as if the nature of the printed codex is the only thing that makes its contents possible. In an absurd extension of the McLuhanesque position about media and messages, they mount arguments which blur the distinction between text and container, and insist that what a book does can be done in no other medium; that the physical characteristics of the object define the book. To them, the book's physicality has made information, or knowledge, widely available and predicated a cultural revolution. To others, print is important because it is only the book which can be read in the bath,[3] annotated in the margins or stained with curry.

But the book's physicality presents limitations. Now that there are other ways to communicate, the need to carry words around in discrete, bulky – and relatively expensive – objects seems decidedly 'olde worlde'. Like it or not, the printed object constrains a book's distribution, increases its cost and makes information and knowledge less accessible than some other media forms. In a world in which finding information involves a little googling and some astute reading (albeit perhaps requiring a new sort of literacy), the idea of having to browse through hundreds of hard copy pages, or consult an incomplete index in a heavy artefact is a bit quaint. What's more, the required book may not be immediately available, or even still in print. At a time when information flows at the velocity of your choice, printed books are an unnecessary speedbump. Despite this, the printed book is still embraced by many; it is seen as easily readable, fixed in nature, permanent, accessible and cheap. Let's consider those characteristics one at a time.

⏭ I can't read on a screen

For the moment, nothing beats a book for readability. Well designed fonts, attractive layout and heavy ink on quality paper all make for a pleasurable reading experience. What's more, books are self-contained; they don't need batteries (although they do require a source of light) and the 'turning page' interface is, if not perfect, perfectly integrated with the 'way we do things'. Some argue that a book's readability is as much about 'touch' as it is about sight. Professor of media studies Tara Brabazon suggests that 'reading is multi-sensory, not only working the ciliary muscles within our eye sockets, but also our fingertips'.[4] Others suggest that with a book, 'the reader is the interface' and the 'haptic feedback' provided by turning pages and the layout of a physical book aids readability and reading.[5] While possibly true, the lack of haptic feedback doesn't seem to have affected the popularity of other media forms. People with internet access now spend more time online than watching television.[6] And given that most of the internet is still text-based, most of that time is spent reading. On a screen. As I suggested in Chapter 3, a shift is occurring in how and what we read. However, it's not universal; for longer forms of text, many people still prefer the tactility and readability of print on paper.

But electronic displays are getting better. Whilst champions of print argue that they are still not as good as ink on paper, it is a huge leap to suggest that they never will be. Similar arguments have been made with other media forms. Proponents of film, for example, have long argued that digital video will never replace 35 mm celluloid; an argument that appears to have been largely lost. The anguished cry from type-perfectionists deriding the threat of computerised publishing processes is but a distant memory. The art of setting type mechanically, and producing galley proofs is long gone. And while it's improbable that an electronic device will exactly replicate the characteristics of paper, something will emerge that most people will accept as good enough. We'll look at the latest contender in Chapter 7.

▶▶ The more things change

Readability isn't the only feature of books. John Updike suggests that 'books have edges'.[7] As well as the edges of its cover, printed books are the physical embodiment of a particular moment in time. Once printed, they cannot be changed. Books are fixed, the ideas within them are preserved for all time. Such permanence has its merits; it means that ideas can be written down, looked up, referred to and engaged with in the certain knowledge that what was said, was actually said. In this way, knowledge can progress, each step building 'on the shoulders of giants'. Much of the scholarship of our time is entirely dependent on this process.

But the book's very advantages as pensive, permanent containers of thought are also its greatest disadvantages. Ideas evolve. The world moves on. Anything less would be unacceptable to reflective human beings. Books, unfortunately, don't. Benjamin Spock's child rearing theories hold little water today (and perhaps today's theories will be similarly discredited in a few decades time). The key cookbooks of the 1960s are amusing and make for great newspaper copy, but their recipes are seldom cooked unadorned with a little extra chilli for a 'more contemporary steak diane'. My *1993 SBS World Fact Book* contains very little that is still considered factual and now serves little purpose other than as a timely reminder of the incessant march of history. Similarly, Ian Fleming's novels are touchstones of a former world, where misogyny and excess were celebrated differently to today. *Pride and Prejudice* might be impeccably crafted and far more eloquent than modern chick-lit novels, but our thinking has surely evolved. Today, I'd be king-hit by a Hermes handbag if I dared suggest that 'It is a truth universally acknowledged, that a single man in possession of a good fortune must be in want of a wife.'[8] I'm not for a moment suggesting that novels require updating to be relevant; merely that while fixed as texts, their meanings vary with the prevailing context.

Ideas about how to live our lives change. Books, as fixed and permanent records of particular ideas cannot *within themselves* reflect the evolving nature of thoughts. Literature is reinterpreted through different social filters, the fixedness of the text often surrounded by ongoing critical discourse. With non-fiction, the publisher's escape route is the second (and third etc) edition, or less frequently, the 'thoroughly revised approach to the same idea that reflects what the author is now thinking'. Unfortunately, people don't often buy the second, third or fourth editions of the same book. I might buy a new street directory every five years to cope with the changing toll-roads,[9] but I'm not about to update the print version of my toddler-taming manuals with every new edition.

This can be a problem for authors as well. The fixedness of the printed book assumes a rigidity in the author's thinking. Printed books suggest that the author still thinks that what they have written is correct, even if they no longer believe it. A printed book doesn't allow for the very natural and very human act of *changing one's mind*. As Alain de Botton suggests:

> [Authors] may wish to move away from a particular stance, only to find that they remain permanently identified with it in the public mind. Whereas most of us can hide old photos and destroy our jottings, artists must live alongside the work they have placed in the public realm, even when this work creates an awkward clash with their present aspirations.[10]

Of course, authors must be made accountable for their thinking. Their ideas should be interrogated, their thoughts dissected, their prose criticised, their sources closely examined, their evidence scrutinised for some resemblance to fact. But books don't permit authors to change their minds publicly. If I suddenly wake up and realise that the book is in fact, not dead but merely resting, this book is less than useful. My readers would assume I still held that view and keep citing me in undergraduate essays.

This constrains writers by forcing them to be defensive; or at the very least incredibly careful. Whether this results in different writing is something that has not been formally tested; I guess that only those who shared a wine-laden feast with an author really know what she thinks. Of course, this isn't a problem for readers, the permanence of print gives them accurate points of reference. In fact it underpins much of the way our cultural life is organised; only by recognising and referencing fixed points of view does the wider conversation evolve and develop. But the printed book does build a fence around an author's ideas. Indeed, such constraints reflect the reality of our wider culture. We want things in writing. It's permanent, legally binding and holds the author accountable. So it is with a book. And whilst this may be appropriate in a society where otherwise intelligent people aspire to be lawyers, it may not necessarily be the best approach for ideas.

That's not to say that fixed forms are not possible in new media realms. Electronic archives are exactly that; most people are unable to alter the electronic version of the majority of things they read. Nobody is suggesting that the texts available on Project Gutenberg are any different from the originals; fixity does not require paper.

▶▶| Forever always ends

A decade ago, science fiction writer Bruce Sterling stated in his *Dead Media* manifesto[11] that all media forms are eventually superseded and replaced. He proposed a project to document the totality of dead and dying media forms into a coffee table book called *The Handbook of Dead Media*. In 2006, the *Dead*

Media project appears to be, well, dead. Its website has not been updated for a while, and Sterling seems quite sanguine about its progress. In an interview with the *Irish Times*, he concludes:

> I was hoping to discover some master key to the death of media that was about media. But I reached the conclusion that media don't die because they are media. They die because they are instantiated as physical, technical objects, and their mortality isn't generally related to the fact that they carry messages.[12]

The death of media is inevitable and electronic media forms are particularly susceptible to shuffling off the mortal coil. Such information forms are 'secondary'; they require a device (and often electricity) before they can be used. A film requires a projector, a broadcast signal needs a radio or television. In this increasingly digitised world, everything seems to run off a computer of some description. Because of this, constant format shifting becomes an issue; newer devices are unable to 'speak' with older technologies. My desk drawer is littered with software that my computer cannot run because the programs are too old, or the computer is too new. And along with that software are copies of things I wrote a decade ago using Magic Writer or WordPerfect or some such thing, which can no longer be read.

The mantra is that books don't have this problem. Once printed they can be read forever, by anyone. After all, paper is permanent, and doesn't require batteries. For the most part this is true. But thousands of books live on my bookshelves. Many of them have yellowed in the sun. Some have pages that are stuck together and cannot be prised apart. A few have been ripped up by a three year old in a pique of curiosity. Others have been destroyed by a clumsy elbow knocking a freshly brewed cup of tea or (more likely) a glass of red wine. I even accidentally dropped a copy of *The Tao of Physics* into a toilet in a cheap French hotel. (Make of that what you will.) If the drowned book is out of print, it is gone forever; lost and unable to be retrieved. Because it's pretty hard to back up a book to disc.

And whilst there *is* the dead media problem with the electronic material, there *is now* an awareness of the need to maintain file formats electronically so that future devices can read them. And the great mass of information that can be easily googled is growing exponentially and is unlikely to totally disappear. Digital copies of most things abound and can be easily found. In fact, it's far more likely that a book will disappear because it is out of print. If my copy of *A Brief History of Time* is eaten by the dog, I can probably find a copy of its text on the internet somewhere.[13]

▶▶ I can't get the book

Until recently, books have been the most accessible of media forms. Television and radio have been largely ephemeral; miss the broadcast moment, and it's in the past. Once a film is no longer screened at the local cinema, it too is essentially gone forever; only preserved by reviews or summaries in (you guessed it) books. Books were different. Libraries maintained an archive of sorts; they were the collective wisdom (and otherwise) of humanity. And bookshops have managed to make available enough stock that the illusion of archiving was preserved even in the retail environment.

More recently, those other media forms have found new outlets. Video and DVD releases made films and television shows as widely available as books (and often in the same stores). And newer digital technologies have allowed almost all media forms to be available anytime, anywhere via digital download. In many ways, the book industry has been the slowest to embrace the new possibilities, stubbornly clinging to a model which worked well in the past.

In fact, books now seem to be *less accessible* than other media forms, partly because a lot of books are published. Every year hundreds of thousands of new titles are added to the growing mountain of published books. Of course, bookshops don't have the shelving to carry all these titles, and publishers don't have the warehouse space to hold copies for very long. So for many consumers, the actual selection of titles may not be very large (particularly in smaller towns or in the suburbs).

Five minutes away from my house is one of Sydney's biggest teaching hospitals. On the other side of which is our second biggest university. But there is no bookshop nearby. The university has a bookshop, but despite a broadening range of general interest books, tertiary texts are its main focus. There *used* to be a reasonable bookshop in the local shopping mall, but it closed a few months ago. Another bookshop used to trade its wares in the main shopping street for two decades. (Before it closed down in 2005, I was still waiting on word about a book I ordered in 1985!)

There *are* a couple of second-hand bookshops. One is a rambling chaotic throwback that book-tragics reminisce about (hoping to stumble serendipitously upon a rare first edition). The other is a more brutally efficient and well-ordered place, run by sharp-edged staff. It manages to survive by remaining open late enough for the cinema crowd to do a post-movie browse.

The demise of the local independent bookshop is a global phenomenon. London's Charing Cross Road used to be *the* street of books, with 84 Charing Cross Road perhaps the most famous address in bookselling. For years, it was the home of Marks & Co, and immortalised in an eponymous novel by Helene Hanff, then a Hollywood movie starring Anne Bancroft. The shop came to epitomise what bookshops should be, and in Hanff's novel, the central character struck up a transatlantic friendship centred around a love of hard-to-get titles. Eighty-four Charing Cross Road is no longer a bookshop. Marks & Co left in 1970, to be replaced by Covent Garden Records and is now part of the All

Bar One pub franchise. And Charing Cross Road itself, once the epicentre of British bookselling is slowly being transformed into just another London street, with smaller independent bookshops closing to make way for global chainstores, and supermarkets. Waterstones, Zwemmers Art and Silver Moon all closed with the new millennium, and while stalwarts Foyles and Blackwells remain, the old Charing Cross Road is no more. The Murder One Crime Bookshop moved to smaller premises in 2005, and Comic Showcase closed in early 2006. In their place, at 122 is a branch of the American *Borders* chain; the independents being unable to pay the increasingly high central London rents.[14]

In America, 'bookstore owners note that the brutal business has claimed some of the nation's most famous independent book stores, including Cody's Books on Telegraph Avenue in Berkeley, California, and WordsWorth Books on Harvard Square in Cambridge, Massachusetts. Most recently, Coliseum Books, a famed New York bookstore, announced it was closing for the second time in its 30-year history – this time for good.' One store survived by removing most of the book objects, instead emphasising the community and conversation around particular books. 'We had 10 000 or 13 000 books in the store,' said Gary Kleiman (owner of BookBeat in Fairfax, California). 'Now we have maybe 1500.'[15] By ordering in books when required by customers, and getting a liquor licence, Kleiman is selling as many books as before and has a lot more customers, with most of his profits coming from the cafe.

Such innovation has yet to reach my suburb. If I want to buy a new book, I have to drive to the closest suburban megamall, or go into the city. The mall has franchise outlets of varying quality, discount superstores which sell half-price books between baby toys and laundry powder and a branch of the multinational book mega-store brand which together with Starbucks and Gap makes shopping in Singapore not much different from shopping in San Jose.

The rise of the book superstore has been blamed for the blockbuster mentality of modern day publishing. It would be nice to think that the blockbuster model allowed a handful of successes to subsidise the publication of other book titles; which may not rack up the requisite sales in the short term, but would build both the backlist and reputation of the publisher in the long term. Unfortunately this does not appear to be happening. Epstein argues that the demise of the independent urban bookseller, replaced by the suburban book superstore has reinforced the dominance of a handful of blockbuster titles, and further marginalised the more literary author:

> The mall bookstores were now paying the same rent as the shoestore next door and were bound by the same fiscal rules. They needed recognisable products that sold on impulse. This meant books by brand-name authors with their armies of loyal readers or by celebrities who pitched their books on the morning television shows ...[16]

And while the big superstores have more titles in stock, blockbusters dominate their sales figures. In his Authors Guild report, David Kirkpatrick[17] cites an internal Barnes & Noble memo which outlines the following:

- 30 per cent of superstore revenue comes from so-called 'frontlist' titles
- 20 per cent of frontlist sales comes from 100 titles
- 20 per cent of backlist revenues comes from 500 titles
- the top titles are known as 'NOS' or Never Out of Stock and include '*Windows for Dummies*, the *Seven Habits* books, cookbooks, mass market books, bestsellers, and self-help books – perennials and books-of-the-moment'
- at Barnes & Noble and at Borders, the vast majority of titles in stock sell fewer than two copies a year.

Kirkpatrick describes the stock held as

> essentially wallpaper ... You come to hang out, but then
> you buy. Along with armchairs, bagels and cappuccino,
> the library-like atmosphere attracts shoppers. The actual
> spending patterns of superstore customers, however,
> are quite different from what the impressive statistics
> about books ordered would lead you to think. In super-
> stores, people buy in a narrower range of titles than they buy
> at independents.[18]

As a study in usefulness, I thought I would try to buy a book
called *When Books Die* which had been favourably reviewed in
the Saturday papers. The franchises had never heard of it, and
it wasn't available at the megastore. The friendly independent
didn't stock it either, and it was only the big Japanese bookseller
in the city that had stock. At the same time, I looked for copies
of various Booker Prize winners and Don DeLillo novels with
varying degrees of success. All of which didn't prove anything
except that the totally comprehensive bookshop does not exist.
At least in the real world.

The *Sydney Morning Herald* recently started a book blog and
bookclub, inviting readers to contribute to online discussion
about a particular title. The first book chosen was *Little Big Man*
by Thomas Berger. Unfortunately, as readers discovered, '*Little
Big Man* is not kept in stock by the Australian distributor!!!
This means that bookshops are very unlikely to have it on their
shelves. Customers will need to special order the title and the
Australian distributor will then order it from the UK ...'[19]

Ironically, new technologies offer better opportunities to
source and buy books. Amazon.com is the most obvious example,
where the illusion of a totally comprehensive collection is the
main attraction. Point your favourite web browser at the Amazon
website, and everything that is being published (and much that
is no longer published) is at your beck and call. Of course, this

isn't entirely the case. Complex copyright laws ensure that even Amazon is not complete. And those of us who are not stateside need to reconcile their purchase with the long wait (and high price) of shipping internationally. How much better would it be if the book you ordered from Amazon's infinite catalogue could immediately appear on your desk, minutes after you click on it. But that's a story for another chapter.

▶▶❙   Libraries

Of course, bookshops can't carry everything. That's why we have libraries. But even they are changing. It's not unusual for the local suburban library to have more computers than books, and their catalogue contains as much electronic media as print. One librarian suggested on the Publib email list that 'according to our library's statistics, video/DVD circ makes up 60% of our annual circulation'.[20]

In the book universe, the British Library is Mecca; a physical treasure trove of literary delights. Whilst its existence as a library in its own right came about relatively recently,[21] its constituent parts include the British Museum's Department of Printed Books whose history can be traced back to 1793. Within its collection are historical treasures including copies of the *Magna Carta* and the *Gutenberg Bible*, and visitors can peruse a fascinating display of early manuscripts that showcase key parts of the library's collection in a suitably darkened gallery. For booklovers, the British Library is a temple in which they can worship; a place where books are central to the institution's very existence.

It also serves as the national printed archive, and is an institution of legal deposit, whereby all UK publishers are legally required to send one copy of each of their publications within one month of publication.[22] No items collected under the terms of legal deposit are to be disposed of. As a result, there are over 150 million works in the collection, making it one of the largest in the world and taking up over 600 kilometres of shelf space.

The library building itself is fairly new, its Euston Road site having been developed in the 1990s. You enter via what could be the foyer of a modern opera house (or mid-market hotel). A huge atrium with a reception desk greets readers as they walk in. Instead of a giant Marc Chagall painting, the backdrop to the reception area is a tower of old books stacked behind glass and visible from the entire atrium area. It's impossible to tell what those books actually are; they're too far away to easily read the spines, but one can only guess that they're not books that are often requested by readers. And there's not a trace of irony in the display. For booklovers, the objects on view represent everything good about books. Permanent, tangible items filled with knowledge written by the greatest minds of the time, and permanently preserved for humanity's benefit. For me, the glass tower more closely resembled a prison, a cage in which knowledge is locked up, undoubtedly kept safe from the elements, but also kept safe from the riff-raff who might dare have some use for it.

The library itself reflects that glass cage. In order to read its books, one has to register as a reader. This process of registration seems harder than obtaining a credit card. I was lucky, I had university accreditation which let me pass relatively smoothly through the identification process, and I was issued with a reader's pass, a plastic photo ID that allowed me access to the library's reading rooms for the next couple of years. Each reading room has a security guard who gives your pass a cursory glance and waves you through. Of course, because the library's collections are precious, most personal items are not permitted into the reading rooms. Small items placed in clear plastic bags (which security staff can inspect easily) are allowed. You can take laptop computers, but other items are to be placed in lockers.

The reading rooms themselves are vast characterless rooms; consisting of row upon row of desks, most of which are occupied by people tapping away at their computers. There aren't many books available for browsing; each of the rooms I visited had few shelves for open inspection. Instead, the collection is accessed by filling in 'material order' forms and submitting those order requests at the appropriate desks. Staff then fill those requests; presumably by entering those 600 kilometres of holdings and finding the appropriate book from the vast collection beneath. The average delivery time for a normal book stored onsite (and some books are still not held in the Euston Road facility) is 70 minutes. Which isn't really too bad. For 1973.

The British Library exemplifies the problem with the book as an object. In the twenty-first century, it is hardly the most accessible and usable format for obtaining information. It's not the library's fault that it takes over an hour to find a book. There are significant physical demands in maintaining and organising 100 million objects, each weighing a couple of kilograms and taking up a fair chunk of space.

Utilising that space more efficiently has resulted in some libraries equipping themselves with robots. The University of British Columbia in Canada stores 30 per cent of its collection in what it calls ASRS (Automated Storage and Retrieval System). Instead of allowing patrons to browse shelves of books, the books are stored in specially designed bins and accessed by a machine, dramatically reducing the 'space between the shelves' and increasing the library's capacity.

And it doesn't stop once the book is delivered. Having actually received the book, the reader faces the daunting task of finding particular content, often within a comparably fragile volume which must be handled with kid gloves. (The reading rooms have padded bookrests which must be used for particularly vulnerable books.) The problem of damaged books is not limited to the British Library. Books are not forever; they are fragile, they break, they fade and if not treated with care, they are no more permanent than the digital forms that booklovers can be so dismissive of. I recently tried to buy two hardbacks as gifts, but the local superstore only had one copy of each. And they both had severely damaged covers. I was offered a small discount and a shrug, which suggested to me that damaged stock was a fact of life. One independent bookseller wrote on her blog: 'The issue of damaged books became a major one, actually threatening to put us out of business.'[23]

So it's no surprise that the British Library (like many others) is embarking on a program of digitisation and making its collection available via less arduous modes of delivery. For example, it is now possible on its Treasures in Full service to view copies of classic texts via the world wide web. The *Gutenberg Bible* and Folio editions of *Shakespeare* can be browsed in this way. A similar project called Turning the Pages makes 15 classic books (ranging from *Leonardo da Vinci's Sketchbook* to the *Diamond Sutra*) viewable in a similar manner. The library's policy seems to be a tacit acknowledgment of the inherent limitations of the book form. Not only is accessibility mooted as a key policy imperative, but preservation is also identified as a driving factor in the process. Perhaps the central glass-enclosed tower of books stands as a monument to the past, a gesture towards a time when the object of the book was the cornerstone of knowledge; a time that even the British Library seems to agree has come and gone.

▶▎ Don't call me cheap

Arguments over accessibility also hinge around the cost of books. Which booklovers assure me is cheap. For 20 bucks, they say, I can escape for a few hours with Jason Bourne on a cold-war adventure through Europe. Try doing that with any of the new-fangled technologies. But removing the object can only make books cheaper. We had a look at some numbers in the previous chapter; while those numbers may not represent all books, I suspect that they point in the right direction. I'm no accountant, but it does cost *something* to print and bind books; and then some more again to ship a book from that factory in southern China.

I grew up with a copy of the *World Book Encyclopedia* in the living room. It had 20 or so volumes, and was supplemented with annual year books designed to provide a modicum of contemporary data. I have no idea what the actual cost of those books were; but they were expensive. Not as expensive as *Britannica*, which only the school library could afford, but expensive enough that we had to treat the hard bound volumes with respect and the constant reminder from our parents that they were for our educational benefit.

The *World Book* was a big part of my life; I flipped through the volumes alphabetically, learnt thousands of factoids, most of which I was destined to forget, and copied chunks of text uncritically into school projects. I marvelled at the heft of the books themselves, and was entranced by those entries that had special features; transparent overlays which built up the various organs, bones and blood vessels of the human body for example.

Today, the *World Book* comes on two shiny circles of plastic and is *free* when you buy some consumer level computers. It contains, not just millions of words, but hours of historically significant video clips and audio sound bites that would have had my primary school teachers salivating. It's connected to the internet, so that up-to-date information is a click away; and is powered by both a useful search engine, and a number of means of browsing the information to allow for serendipitous discovery. I doubt if many people buy a hard copy of the *World Book Encyclopedia* anymore. Naysayers might argue that the cost of a computer skews the comparison, but a cheap PC bundled with the latest *World Book* CD or DVD-ROM costs less in real terms than the last printed edition.[24] The *World Book* store sells the 2006 print edition for US$989. The CD-ROM for Windows is US$23. Last time I checked, US$966 buys a pretty decent computer.

The market for printed encyclopedias has essentially disappeared. Most have reinvented themselves as CD-ROMs or DVD-ROMs and are sold for a fraction of the price. Others are experimenting with online delivery mechanisms and exploring subscription models to generate revenue. Irrespective of which business model will eventually win out, this reference space is one in which the printed book has essentially died. The advantages of multimedia and searchability; combined with the type of reading required to glean something useful from a reference work has meant that arguments about readability are seldom heard.

To the current generation of school children, an encyclopedia is accessed by sitting at a computer screen and navigating with mouse and keyboard through a range of audio, visual and textual content. In every physical sense, it is as different from the traditional encyclopedia as it is possible to imagine. Yet the *idea* of an encyclopedia remains. *World Book* and *Britannica* still employ hundreds of researchers, writers and designers who compile the essential knowledge of the western world. That content evolves and grows; building on decades (or in the case of *Britannica*) centuries of history and tradition. Discarding (or reconfiguring) the object has saved the encyclopedia. The new media format allows far more content than the printed book; the manufacturing and distribution costs have been significantly reduced; and arguably the new media technologies have allowed a greater democratisation of knowledge. It's hard to believe that the same formula could not apply elsewhere; that *all* books cannot be delivered far more cheaply if the object is reinvented, or even discarded.

Part of the problem with books as objects is that they have a particular product life cycle. As we have seen, publishers must guess how many copies of a particular book will sell and print and store those copies in their warehouse until sold. If they sell out, a reprint is ordered. If not, the remaining books are remaindered, sold cheaply to discount outlets, or pulped. Thus, every book has a 'natural' life cycle which is determined by the publisher's business model.[25] New media proponent and *Guardian* columnist, Jeff Jarvis suggests that books are where 'words go to die'.[26] He argues that once a book is printed and sold (or pulped), the text disappears. Once the publisher has decided that it is no longer profitable for a book to be kept in the warehouse, then it essentially no longer exists. Except in second-hand bookstores.

There must be a better way to communicate the essence of books; to tell the stories and get people talking about the ideas. Book culture needs to be dragged into the twenty-first century. It's been a long time since we've waited on the mail boat for news from home; in this day and age, it would be unthinkable to communicate only via letter. And yet, that's where book culture remains; chained to an object that dramatically limits its potential.

▶▶ If not books, then what?

Ask a booklover why books are important and the answer is more often than not a conflation of various ideas. Booklovers love reading. They adore stories. They revel in the fact that publishers and editors have the ability to ensure some kind of quality control over what they are reading. They embrace the mythic idea of writers and writing. They practically drool in bookshops. And they are wedded to the *object* that is the book. The booklover doesn't generally distinguish those various elements, but sees the book as a holistic combination; one which is destroyed should any single piece of the puzzle be removed.

The object is loved for a number of reasons; proponents argue that the printed codex has served us well, and such 'no-tech' solutions are flexible, adaptable and readable. They say that new media forms have few advantages and lack the romance of the printed page. For the most part, the arguments seem valid. Despite widespread internet usage, reading on a computer monitor is still not easy for some, particularly if it requires sitting at a desk. A portable computer of some sort might be better; but to date, there has been no magic bullet which combines the enchanted elements made possible by the printed book.

But the elusive combination is neither impossible nor improbable. And it's clear that the book must have a digital future if it is to be reborn. Indeed, the reality is that books almost invariably begin life as digital files; written using Microsoft Word or something similar. And the entire production process remains digital until the object is produced. Behind every printed book sits its electronic facsimile which publishers delight in hiding from its customers.

Of course, the path to a digital future has a past and a present. Previous efforts to move on from the printed book are replete with missteps, false dawns and red herrings. The next chapter explores some efforts to separate the book from its object.

▶▶| CHAPTER 7.
Reconfigurations

I own to you frankly that I do not believe (and the progress of electricity and modern mechanism forbids me to believe) that Gutenberg's invention can do otherwise than sooner or later fall into desuetude as a means of current interpretation of our mental products ... Our grandchildren will no longer trust their works to this somewhat antiquated process, now become very easy to replace by phonography.

Octave Uzanne (1894)[1]

You can think about new media technologies in two ways. The first is to understand the new modes of production and distribution as a means to extend the reach of existing media properties. Like distributing episodes of *Lost* via the internet, or making Louis Armstrong's catalogue available via the iTunes store, or putting the *New York Times* on the web. Let's call that the *new old media*. The second approach – which we can call the *new new media* – looks for things that previously haven't been possible. Rather than privileging existing media products, the *new new media* encourages entirely different forms of engagement; it blurs production and consumption; highlights the tension between interactivity and narrative and shifts the emphasis from the content to the user. Examples include so-called citizen journalism, social networks and videogames. It is the new new media that scares the traditional institutions and has the pundits in a lather, with breathless suggestions of how YouTube means the death of television, Instapundit the end of journalism, MySpace the death of the pub and Google the death of books (whoops).

But, of course, the two forms are not exclusive; the new old media and the new new media can (and do) happily co-exist. In fact, some might argue that without the former, the latter would have nothing to talk about. We live in a time when users have the luxury of choice; many have left behind decades-old cultural habits and simply cherry-pick from various available media forms. They also have the luxury of being able to talk back in public; the new media technology makes the human conversation possible and visible. Media corporations who staunchly defend the old ways without understanding the new media environment are being stupidly stubborn. Traditional media approaches may not die out immediately, but they must find a way to co-exist with the new; or generational change will ensure their demise.

The book industry is no different. In previous chapters, I've suggested that the way to save the book is to kill the object, and replace it. But should the approach be new new media, or new old media? Should those book objects be replaced by something completely different; unrecognisable as books as the technological possibilities allow for reconfigurations of reading and writing? Or should we merely repackage existing books, and use the new networks as a means to market and distribute the same texts that we have lovingly called books for so long?

▶▶| Giant leaps

For the moment, it's worth examining some new new media approaches to the book; exploring innovative alternatives to print.

In the early 1990s, the book industry took its first tentative steps into the new media with the adoption of multimedia CD-ROM production. For a brief moment, some genres were re-cast as shiny plastic discs. Children's books and reference titles in particular were reconfigured with animations, music, movies and point-and-click interaction. Some sold well, but problems of compatibility with rapidly changing computer operating systems, high development costs, and little attraction beyond an initial novelty value saw publishers largely discard the CD-ROM as a failed experiment. A couple of examples follow.

In 1992, the Australian government launched a multilateral cultural policy called *Creative Nation*. Part of that policy was a recognition that computer-based multimedia technologies would be central to Australia's cultural future. Whilst acknowledging that broadband would eventually provide a natural solution to distribution issues with such media forms, it provided funding for an interim publishing medium, the CD-ROM. Ten titles were published under the auspices of the *Creative Nation* project, and distributed free to schools and libraries. Whilst their quality varied, they were largely well-received[2] and provided an alternative to the mainly American multimedia material that was available at the time. But today, the project is largely forgotten, and seems to have been of dubious longer-term significance.

The Voyager Company reconfigured books by such luminaries as Marvin Minksy and Marshall McLuhan in a series of classy multimedia adaptations that explored the interactive possibilities of the new media form. To many, Voyager titles, published as CD-ROMs, represented everything that was attractive about the possibilities of multimedia. They combined key texts with new approaches; allowing readers to have an author's books explained and expounded on by the author. Some Voyager titles explored the more obscure interactive possibilities of the media form; titles like The Residents' *Freak Show* providing a new publishing canvas for creativity. But it wasn't enough. By the late 1990s, Voyager no longer existed, and the rights to its catalogue of titles (which numbered 500 in various media forms)[3] had been sold.

It didn't take long for the promise of CD-ROMs to fade. For a brief moment, they were the shining hope of a new publishing industry, combining the best of all media forms into a unified whole. Book publishers, not wanting to be left behind, were keen to explore their possibilities. But very few sold as stand-alone products on their merits. Before long, the CD-ROM became a marketing device; bundled in packs of 10 with new computers, or stapled onto glossy hard cover books as a bonus gift.

With the notable exception of encyclopedias, the CD-ROM was a passing new media phase. As a result of this 'failure', book publishers remained sceptical about the new media, and for the most part, have focused on selling printed books. Even the rise and rise of the internet has seen only grudging adoption by the book trade. Today, publishing websites are used as simple marketing tools and the ability to utilise the *conversational* potential of the internet has largely been ignored. Apart from a few educational publishers who add value to their textbooks with interactive online elements, publisher websites are bareboned and stingy. Extracts are uncommon, opportunities to communicate with authors mostly non-existent, and even purchasing possibilities are rare. Rather than allow book-buying from their own sites, most publishers direct would-be buyers to third party sellers. This reticence to embrace the new media extends to other electronic formats; book publishers still hesitate to look beyond the printed object. The CD-ROM experiment is regularly held up as evidence that the old media forms will outlive the new.

▶▶| Hypertext – neither here nor there

Outside the book trade, others saw the computer as a logical place for creating and disseminating new literary forms. The more revolutionary approaches suggested that traditional books could be replaced with new ways of writing and reading; centred around *hypertext*. The idea of hypertext suggests the creation of non-linear texts that allow users to create their own pathways through a narrative of sorts. To book readers, the simplest form of hypertext can be equated to the footnote, but it has come to mean much more than a simple link to an external text. The word itself was coined by Ted Nelson in the 1960s as 'non-sequential writing – text that branches and allows choices to the reader, best read at an interactive screen. As popularly conceived, this is a series of text chunks connected by links which offer the reader different pathways.'[4] Hypertext can be traced from Vannevar Bush's 1945 article 'As We May Think',[5] through projects such as Doug Engelbart's NLS system of the late 1960s, Nelson's own Project Xanadu concept and Apple's Hypercard software which shipped free with Macintosh computers in the late 1980s.[6]

Hypertext is used in popular products such as computerised training manuals, help systems and reference works such as encyclopedias or databases. But while the approach works in non-fiction spaces, it has failed to gain much more than a small cult following elsewhere. The reasons are manifold. Reading a hypertext fiction involves challenges not normally required of a book reader. In an old-fashioned book, the intricacies of reading are internalised, the reader is free to explore nooks and crannies beyond the text at their own leisure. Or not. In a hypertext, the reader *must* engage in narrative somersaults. For example, Michael Joyce's *Twelve Blue*[7] has no beginning; the reader is presented with a grid of jagged lines, nodes which link to pages of text. It also has no overt storyline; the grid represents the foundation of the text and is the primary means of narrative navigation. As a result there are several main characters (each of whom can have different names) and several entangled storylines. It's interesting the way an arty *Biennale* installation is interesting; intellectually challenging but not necessarily compelling. Reading *Twelve Blue* is hard work (only partly due to the use of blue on blue text), and there's not a lot that motivates the casual reader to keep (hyper) reading. It turns out that despite the pioneering work of people like Joyce, hypertexts, so-called interactive fictions and the like, are as appealing to most people as poetry.

A cultural inertia exists when it comes to a particular type of storytelling. We prefer stories with beginnings, middles and ends. Most attempts to reduce reader interaction to broad narrative choices have failed, which suggests that those choices are the least important part of interactivity. While we are happy to have faster, more complex narratives, and even become (dare I say it) intertextual, there is still room for what Jay David Bolter calls anti-reading,[8] the type of (apparently) passive reading which allows the author to take the lead. And it seems I'm not alone. Every time I show someone a branching hypertext-fiction, they mutter excitedly about remembering *choose your own adventure* books from their childhood and grab the mouse. Five minutes later, their eyes have glazed over and they're hunting for people.com.

▶▶ǀ   World wide web

At one point in the 1990s, hypertext was touted as the future of writing. It represented the death of linearity, the victory of interactivity over passive acceptance of a narrative and the simultaneous death of the author and rise of the reader. Proponents enthused about the new computerised 'writing spaces' and evoked Roland Barthes' notion of an 'ideal textuality', a text 'composed of blocks of words linked electronically multiple paths, chains, trails in an open-ended, perpetually unfinished textuality'.[9]

'Hypertext' became loaded with meanings. Far from being merely a new structure for writing, it encompassed the idea of the network, the further blurring of production and consumption and the total reconfiguration of intellectual life. The rhetoric surrounding the emergence of hypertextual systems and the demise of the book proposed no less than a revolution in ways of thinking. It painted book culture as self-contained, closed and representing an impenetrable barrier behind which the author resided with his ideas. Hypertext would change all that:

> [The end of the book] signal[s] not simply the demise of the bookmark industry or relief from the dangers of papercuts, but a way of thinking about the way we organize, conceive and imagine the world in which we live. To think of the world not as a Book but as a hypertext is to conceive of it as a heterogeneous, mutable, interactive and *open-ended* space where meaning is inscribed between signs, between *nodes*, and between readers, not enclosed between the limits of a front and back cover, or anchored to some conceptual spine called the author.[10]

The world wide web turned hyperbolic theory into realistic practice. When Tim Berners-Lee designed the protocols for the world wide web, hypertext formed its fundamental structural approach and allowed web users to easily move from one webpage to another. The mainstream adoption of the web browser meant that using hypertext, by 'web-surfing', is now as much a cultural habit as watching television. At first blush, the world wide web *is* the hypertext revolution without the ideological baggage. But whilst it is part of everyday life, the web has not replaced *books*. The web, for the most part, still happens much too quickly to do what books do. Instead, it provides an alternative to printed newspapers and magazines. A webpage mirrors the length of articles in such publications, and (as suggested in Chapter 3) the web's availability and currency makes the print forms essentially extinct. Apart from making the conversation more visible, hypertext also speeds it up; when books ideally should slow things down.

There is another revolution that would use books as a starting point, incorporating the accumulated wisdom of print culture. In this broader vision, the contents of printed books would be made available on the network. As well as leaping from text to text and searching for topics of interest, readers would be able to annotate, comment and reflect in a public forum of ideas (in a manner common to the world wide web, but underpinned with content from published books). But the world wide web does not do that ... yet. The Google Book Search project seeks to do just this, creating what *Wired* editor Kevin Kelly calls the liquid version of books,[11] snippets of texts, linked together and totally searchable. At present Google is negotiating with libraries, publishers and authors' associations, but its vision is clear. It hopes to make the contents of books searchable online; with a view to eventually making their entire texts available electronically.[12]

▶▶| Networked books

An alternative notion of interactivity involves the reader as a writer. Brian Eno suggested that 'interactivity' is the wrong word; and that 'unfinished' is better.[13] The 'networked book' represents an interesting approach to that idea, and a more measured development of blogs and wikis. A project from the Institute for the Future of the Book,[14] the networked book is a model for a new (virtual) object that relies on building a relationship between the author and her readership. Like the more common wiki, the networked book allows readers to contribute to an evolving text. Unlike wikis, the starting point is a completely authored text, and reader contributions are limited to general critique and comment which the author can then choose to incorporate.

According to the project's instigators, the networked book is

> a hypertextual kind of book. It has linkages within it, and linkages leading out and leading in the larger network. A networked book is social. It incorporates feedback mechanisms and discussion platforms in its overall structure ... most importantly, a networked book is organic and is more about process than product.

All of which is almost meaningless and pretty much describes all manner of electronic communications on the internet, from forums through to wikis. Luckily there's more, and the project differentiates itself from other less well-defined forms: 'it has boundaries, even though in the case of a networked book, those boundaries are highly porous. Boundaries that are meaningful.'[15]

As well as throwing the idea around, the institute developed *gamertheory*, a networked book.[16] It was 'authored' by Mackenzie Wark, and made available and open to feedback for much of 2006. Wark wrote the book in precise snippets; it has nine chapters of 25 sections, each 200 words long and presented in a faux index card style. Comments for each section are posted alongside, and the design encourages a non-linear dipping into the various byte-sized (sorry) chunks. Having incorporated reader input, a print version of *gamertheory* was published by Harvard University Press. It is a possible future for the book, but it's not the only one.

▶▶| What about videogames?

Australian book publisher Michael Duffy quit the business in late 2005, farewelling the trade in an op-ed piece in the *Sydney Morning Herald*. His parting words were 'My prediction is that the next big decline in reading will occur when someone invents good computer games for adults. I don't know what the game version of *Pride and Prejudice* or a Michael Connelly novel or a biography of Mao will look like, but I think they're possible. And I suspect I'll be buying them.'[17] For the most part I agree with him (books are no longer central to our ideas, it's getting harder to be a successful independent publisher), but I think he's wrong about games. They will not replace books because they are a different thing entirely. There are already good games for adults. Yes, many of them are sports simulations or interactive gangster movies. But there are other sub-genres which involve narrative ideas, problem solving and don't require killing. *The Sims, Spore, Civilization, Grim Fandango* and *Myst* spring to mind.

My long-suffering partner bought me a Nintendo DS Lite for my birthday-just-gone. And only impending deadlines have prevented me from totally succumbing to the charms of Mario as he battles to rescue Princess Peach. *Super Mario Bros* has a plot of sorts, but it isn't a book, nor does it pretend to be. It's a game; one that involves twitching muscles and a little puzzle-solving and it succeeds in the same way that *Solitaire* does: by providing enough reward to be comforting and sufficient difficulty to be an addictive challenge.

The growing sophistication of portable gaming devices probably adds to the illusion that they represent an alternative to books. Which they do, but not in the way that Duffy suggests. Books and videogames appeal to distinct desires. They do different things. Whilst they might compete for the same attention-span and dollar-spend, the experience of gameplay has little in common with that of reading a book. Despite game theorists arguing that *Grand Theft Auto* represents the direction for new interactive fiction (you *are* the central character), games are something else entirely. A good game requires gameplay. And no amount of ludic analysis or arbitrary stick-on narratives can disguise a bad game. Chess doesn't *need* its feudal context to work as a game. And *Tetris* is fun and addictive without a background story of any sort. Of course, sophisticated storylines can add to the enjoyment of a game, and the introduction of interesting characterisations and relationships is not a bad thing. But they can't make up for a boring game.

Whilst some (like myself) would welcome more literary elements into their gaming experience (better characterisations, plot development), the game version (like the film version), of *Pride and Prejudice* will not replace the book version. As I suggested in Chapter 2, the act of reading requires a different type of engagement; it internalises the activity, allowing the reader to immerse herself in an imagined universe; to complete the author's work in her own image. A game externalises the responses; demands of the player an overt reaction to what's happening on screen. Readers are not necessarily gamers, nor are gamers necessarily readers.

You might recall the fact that readers are primarily female (see Chapter 3). Gaming is similarly gendered. Go to a writers' festival, any writers' gathering and the halls are lacking in testosterone. Particularly the aroma of youthful male hormones; which are usually to be found shackled to some form of computer game. Go to a gaming lounge in Chinatown (or a consumer electronics show), and you'll see mostly boys. The gender divide makes it pretty clear that books and games do different things. For whatever reason, PlayStation and Xbox (or football, cars and downloading porn) are a more attractive proposition for males; just as novels are a more attractive proposition for females; which reinforces my sense that Michael Duffy's instinct about games replacing books is misplaced.

The networked, collaborative book is also a furphy. Experiments like *gamertheory* may be of academic interest, but don't attract much attention beyond the new breed of anoraks with 'creative commons' logos tattooed to their inner thighs. For the moment, these giant leaps are all virtual red herrings. Whilst hypertexts, networked books and the dubious interactive delights of other media forms might one day reflect those characteristics of a *book culture*, they are an unnecessary diversion. Old-fashioned book content does not have to be reinvented. The only thing required to save book culture is to kill the object. And the easiest way to do that is to embrace a digital future; to take the contents of the books we have always had, and make them all available digitally as ebooks.

▶▶ If at first you don't succeed

But haven't ebooks been a failure? Naysayers always seem to remember Stephen King. In March 2000, King released a new novella called *Riding the Bullet*. His publisher, Simon & Schuster didn't publish it as a printed book, but instead made it available for download on the web. More than half a million copies were downloaded and the surrounding buzz was astonishing. All of a sudden, ebooks had arrived, and book publishers were keen to embrace the new future of publishing.[18] Simon & Schuster announced a flurry of digital publishing ventures and other publishers seemed to finally understand the potential of ebooks. King himself announced that his next new media venture would be a serialised novel, *The Plant*. He would bypass his publishers and offer the book direct to his readers; they would download and pay for a chapter at a time. But after six chapters, which had cost readers $7, King announced that he was suspending publication; ostensibly because not enough people were paying for the downloads. Book publishers seemed to welcome King's apparent failure as a victory of sorts; even in the brave new media world, publishers seemed to be necessary. In the longer term though, the failure of *The Plant* was cited as evidence that ebooks themselves were doomed; and that the book's future in print remained certain.

Of course, *The Plant* was not the first ebook; nor was it the last. Many other authors write and publish electronic texts with varying degrees of success. King's effort proved a turning point simply because of his brand; it might have validated the idea of electronic distribution and when it was aborted, the idea that ebooks themselves were a failure was a natural consequence. There was nothing *new new media* about *The Plant*; it was a *new old media* project; it merely dispensed with the object and presented an alternative distribution and payment method from which publishers might have learnt some lessons.

Perhaps the cost per chapter was too high; the overall price for the delivered chapters ended up being more than for a printed paperback book. Early adopters of new media technologies might be willing to squint at a computer screen, but they're not fools, and won't pay more for an inferior reading experience.

Downloaders also suggested that the user experience was problematic; the approach limited the type of device on which the book could be read; and arguably the required display technologies just weren't ready at the turn of the century.

▶▶ꞏ Baby steps

Electronic reading devices have been around for as long as there have been computers with screens, but attempts to replicate the portability, readability and convenience of a book have only been with us for a decade. A flurry of devices emerged around the turn of the century, all sporting (barely) readable liquid crystal screens and the capacity to carry around dozens of text titles. None managed to gain mainstream acceptance, and while a few generated some publisher support, they could never be considered successful. Large computer companies also made a huge effort around this time, with Microsoft and Adobe both pitching their reading software as the digital book solution.

'This is a Story about the Future of Reading' shouted the headline of a four-page colour spread in the January 2000 issue of the now defunct *Brill's Content* magazine. The ad went on to outline how Microsoft Reader would 'revolutionise publishing' with a colour coded timeline that 'represents the best estimates of Microsoft researchers':

2002: PCs and eBook devices offer screens almost as sharp as paper

2005: The sale of eBook titles, eMagazines, and eNewspapers top $1 billion

2006: eBook stands proliferate offering book and periodical titles at traditional bookstores, newstands, airports ...

2009: eBook titles begin to outsell paper in many categories

2012: Electronic and paper books compete vigorously. Pulpo industry ads promote 'Real Books from Real Trees for Real People'

2019: Paper books remain popular as gifts for collectors ...

2020: Webster alters its 1st definition of the word 'book' to refer to eBook titles read on a screen ...

Of course, the benefit of hindsight is a wonderful thing (and reading past predictions of the future is always amusing). But, sitting as we are, a third of the way through Microsoft's 20-year timeline for the electronic book to become ubiquitous, how did they go at playing Nostradamus? The answer has to be 'not very well'.

In 2002, screens were nowhere near as sharp as paper (although they're now getting a lot closer). In 2005, the sales of electronic titles have yet to crack $100 million, let alone the billion predicted.[19] And well into 2007, I have yet to see a single 'ebook stand' anywhere.

What's really happened has been incremental and stuttering. Ebook reading devices began appearing in the late 1990s. In quick succession, the Rocket eBook, the SoftBook, the Franklin eBookman all appeared and found niche markets. Microsoft's reader software competed with a similar product from Adobe, and managed to get a few publishers onboard, but the devices were not yet ready for widespread adoption and the competing formats and lack of publishing support relegated ebook reading to those nerds sufficiently comfortable with the technology to download the appropriate software tweaks.

More recently, e-reading efforts have focused on convergent devices; mobile telephones and personal digital assistants. Their primary purpose is not to deliver ebook texts, but they possess screens with sufficient space to make reading reasonably comfortable. Communities of ebook readers have appeared, and a large range of titles is available for purchase in a number of common formats to feed a demand that is still very much driven by geeky early adopters. But while ebook enthusiasts show unbridled enthusiasm, this represents a very small niche. Most of us still read printed books.

Booklovers cite this 'failure' of the ebook as evidence that the book will not die; that the printed object has so many advantages that it will never be replaced. But cautionary parallels in other industries sound a warning to the traditional book. Technological changes take *longer than we expect*, but with an impact that can be *greater than imagined*.

▶▶| Music – a lesson from not that long ago

Music publishing has a relatively short history when compared to print. Vinyl records emerged in the early twentieth century and with the introduction of commercial radio, sales took off in earnest around World War II. The industry matured into a multi-billion dollar marketing institution that relied for its survival on a combination of finding music talent, buying it and leveraging those assets and creating 'products' in the form of manufactured music celebrities packaged and merchandised to the public. It is clear that for half a century its output has been tightly controlled and manipulated with a deft combination of marketing and production skills.

Like the book publishing industry, the central component of the music publishing industry has been an object. Unlike books, that object has changed a number of times over the last five decades, but until very recently, the industry's success was based on selling a *thing*. That object was originally the vinyl record, which itself changed its size and specification a number of times. Originally spun at 78 revolutions per minute (rpm), playback technology improved to allow acceptable fidelity (and longer playtime – hence the lp or long play) at 33 rpm. It spawned the single, and the time limits defined by the capacity of each side constrained the possibilities of musicians for decades. Records were played on record players; a technology that was fiddly, unreliable and allowed a maximum of 20 minutes or so of uninterrupted music.

Those vinyl records were also hard to produce, heavy to ship, took up enormous amounts of shelf space, broke easily, melted or warped if left out in the sun and were generally a pain. But consumers bought them by the billions because they were all we had. They did, of course, have some tactile attributes which made them attractive to many. Their sheer physical size and the need to protect them inside some kind of packaging led to the creation of album art that was often more intricate than the music on the record itself. Santana's 1974 triple album set *Lotus* is the perfect example; a multi-page multi-colour work of art that folded out from a single square into a veritable patchwork quilt containing psychedelic livery of incredible intricacy.

The audiocassette arrived in the mid to late '60s. An invention of the Dutch Philips company, it was originally intended as a dictation system for secretarial work, but its portability and robustness drew attention from music consumers who wanted to take their music with them. What the cassette taught us is that people were happy with 'good enough'. Audiophiles argued that the fidelity of the audiocassette was inferior to the vinyl record, and they were right. But most people didn't care. The creation of mobile boom boxes and the Sony Walkman, combined with recordability made cassettes popular with many. A generation of teenagers learned to love music by making cassette copies of *Dark Side of the Moon* from their friend's vinyl versions. Record companies released albums on cassette, but for the most part records and cassettes lived an uneasy co-existence; one for home, the other for more mobile situations.

The big shift came in the mid 1980s with the invention of the compact disc (CD). Digital technologies had become affordable, and the CD promised a revolution; the robustness of cassettes, and better fidelity than records, together with longer playing time. It delivered on all counts, and came to dominate the music industry. Whilst some anorak wearers continue to lament the demise of vinyl, the compact disc took over, its advantages clear to most.

The most recent change is the shift from object to non-object. A container for distributing digital music files is no longer required; the global computer network has replaced the need to ship five-inch plastic discs around the globe. While not yet the dominant mode for music purchasing, the chasm has been leapt; a couple of billion songs a year are purchased on legal download services; billions more are being shared on less legitimate peer-to-peer networks; and an entire generation has grown up without having had the dubious pleasure of flipping through the chaos of the sale bins in the CD superstore. Instead they get their music whenever they want via intelligent search algorithms on a ubiquitous network.

The moment has not yet arrived, but the pieces are in place for the most dramatic reshaping of the music industry in – oh – at least 20 years; as the industry stakes its claims and shores up its position, the direction is indisputable, even if the actual outcome (and the winners and the losers) is still up for grabs. It may take some time to play out, but the demise of the object and the rise of the 'heavenly jukebox' is well underway.

Of course, the CD will not totally disappear, but its usage will change. It is likely to fill the role of archiving object; a physical permanence used to reassure us that we actually still have a copy of that ephemeral digital file. And it will be used rather more selectively, both for that archival purpose and perhaps as a tangible gift; a playlist constructed and burnt onto a CD is still a grander gesture than an emailed mp3 file.

The introduction of the iPod and the iTunes store represented the so-called tipping point; an easy to use, end-to-end solution for purchasing, managing and listening to digital music. But the iPod was not the first mp3 player, and the iTunes music store was not the first to provide legitimate digital downloads. Rather, the iPod managed to provide that elusive combination of a 'good enough' technology at a reasonable cost. It was the first to have that necessary mix of ease-of-use, fidelity, portability and relative affordability. The iPod also became a fetish object in its own right. Its design is universally applauded as a thing of beauty and it means that music lovers can transfer their tactile desire away from CD-objects and onto the iPod itself. It took Apple two years to sell a million iPods, and a year to sell a million songs; now it sells that number of iPods in little more than a week and that many songs every few hours.

A similar tipping point for the book as object can be imagined. The reading device will fulfil the requirements of readability, portability and affordability, combined with seamless integration with an electronic book store. I'm not alone in this thinking.[20] *The failure of ebooks to date is not an indication that they will always fail.* To many, it's no longer a matter of *if* the printed book will be displaced, but *when*: 'When something is good enough and close enough to paper for people to say, "I want to use this," then things will change quickly as they have with the iPod.'[21]

Similar stories abound in other sectors. Only a few years ago, photography enthusiasts and amateurs alike were disdainful of the digital camera; they were expensive, chewed up batteries, the image quality was woeful and the idea of photographs stored and viewed on computer screens seemed totally alien. Today the largest film companies on the planet are either out of business or no longer sell film products;[22] the dominant camera manufacturers are electronics companies and those camera companies that haven't adapted to the digital realm have disappeared. What's more, we have all come to love the digital archive for its flexibility and searchability. Consumers have embraced the ability to take a hundred photographs and selectively print in formats from glossy coffee table albums to pseudo oil-paintings. Professionals appreciate the workflow advantages; particularly in speed of transmission and manipulation.

Again, change took a long time to occur and then happened very rapidly. Digital cameras took over a decade to become an overnight success. The first digital cameras appeared in the early 1990s and even by 2002 were not a commonplace consumer item. In the space of a few short years, everything changed and digital cameras now easily outsell film cameras. The first contemporary ebook readers emerged a few years after the first digital cameras. Technologies don't have parallel trajectories, and each has their own challenges to overcome, but the slow, unsteady pace of ebook reader development is not unusual.

Lessons for the book industry might be drawn from how people use digital photography. Virtual images (digital files) did not *replace* analogue hard copy prints. Rather, they *displaced* them; the hard copy process has evolved not disappeared. The 24-hour photo lab is now the instant print photo kiosk in the local chemist or the cheap colour printer in the study. Similarly, ebooks will not replace printed books overnight. Rather, they will take some markets away, and allow others to emerge. People are printing their digital photos selectively; the soft copy is used for organisation and archiving (and more and more communicating and displaying via email or website or flickr.com), the hard copy for display in a physical environment; or as a significant gift. There has been a rethink in the uses for the photograph as object; all of a sudden, glossy calendars and wall-sized canvases have become relatively cheap options. In the book realm, there might be a similar demand for meticulously produced fetish objects from digital downloads.

▸▸▎ Not good enough

But e-reading devices to date have not yet made the grade. As it stands, current display technology is not good enough for most people to read a long text on a screen. Most electronic screens fail to deliver sufficient contrast and resolution to make reading ebooks appealing. But it's naive to believe that this will always be the case. Screen technologies have advanced dramatically in the last few years; the resolution of a mobile phone screen is amazing compared to what was available not that long ago.

Whereas computer monitors in the 1990s had resolutions of around 72 dots per inch (dpi), portable devices can now be purchased with 220 dpi screens; not that far from the 300 dpi of the first laser printers. What's more, newer e-ink technologies hint at even greater possibilities.

And of course, current electronic devices are already more portable than traditional printed books. My phone has a one gigabyte memory card. I can buy titles from ereader.com, which each take up a tiny amount of that memory; allowing me to carry a couple of hundred books in my back pocket. What suffers at the moment is readability. And price.

Detractors of an e-reading future argue that any device which costs a few hundred dollars is simply too expensive to replace the printed book object. They're right in some ways. But as I've suggested previously, books aren't cheap. Our understanding of cost is always strangely skewed: we tend to think that large one-off payments are bigger than a series of smaller ones. So leasing a car at $1500 a month seems cheaper than paying $30000 up front (even if you have to make 24 of those smaller payments). Likewise, owners of $300 DVD players seldom reflect on the fact that their DVD libraries consisting of a mere dozen titles (at $30 a piece) required a greater investment. In this context, even though the instinctive reaction might be otherwise, an e-reading device is a small part of the total investment in reading. I've mentioned this before, but it's worth repeating; individually, books cost very little; cumulatively, they cost heaps. But cultural habits die hard and an e-reading system would have to *seem* comparable in cost to printed books.

⏩ And so to the Sony Reader

At the time of writing, the e-reading device du jour is the Sony Portable Reader, the most recent attempt to create an iPod for reading. Promised for much of 2006, the Portable Reader was finally released in September 2006. It was noted (and notable) because:

- it used new e-ink screen technology;

- it was tied to an online bookshop which featured several large publishers as content providers; and

- it was from a reputable consumer electronics brand.

E-ink technology has been heralded as the panacea for ebook devices. It has high contrast and resolution and unlike traditional notebook computer screens, it is reflective, making the experience much closer to ink on paper. In fact, just like a printed book, it requires ambient light and cannot be read in the dark. What's more, electricity is not required to display an e-ink page; it is only needed to make changes to what is displayed. Power is consumed only when e-book pages are 'turned', which is terrific for battery life. The Sony Portable Reader is not the first commercial product that uses e-ink. It's not even the first Sony product to use it. That honour belongs to the Libre reader, which Sony only sold in Japan. Introduced in 2004, the Libre was only modestly successful.[23] Other manufacturers are also using e-ink and a number of competing devices are slated for imminent release. Where Sony appears to have an advantage is in content provision. Mimicking the iTunes store/iPod relationship, Reader users can purchase from a selection of ebooks at the Sony Connect store. The Reader will hold 75–100 books in its internal memory and its battery should allow it to go a week between charges.

Early reviews of the Portable Reader were mixed. The screen was widely praised for its readability, with a resolution of approximately 170 dpi. But respectable resolution is not the only criterion for an acceptable screen technology, and it seems that by some other criteria, the Reader's screen is still not good enough. The device displays a page of text at a time (in four shades of grey, not colour) and each page is 'turned' by pressing an appropriate button. Unfortunately, each page turn takes about a second and is accompanied by the screen turning to black as it is refreshed. Some claim not to notice this delay, but others complain that it severely disturbs the continuity of the book. Other complaints centre around the device's lack of navigational features. Like a printed book, there is no search function; so one of the much mooted advantages of the electronic book is not present. And unlike a printed book, the slow page-turning problem puts paid to any idea of skimming quickly through its contents.[24]

For the Reader to gain widespread acceptance, it has to offer a price advantage over the printed book. It's not good enough to match the price of print, it has to beat it by a mile. Consider the iPod experience. Whilst iPods themselves can cost a few hundred dollars, they replace an electronic device (a CD player) that was once similarly priced. The Sony Portable Reader costs much the same as an iPod, but it's an *additional* cost; reading a printed book doesn't require an electronic machine, so the Reader starts off with a huge price hurdle to overcome.

Once paid for, iPods can be 'fed' from a number of sources. Users can digitise their existing CD collections for no additional cost. They can fill up with illegal downloads for free. Or they can legally buy songs from the iTunes store, which offers some advantages over a physical CD. As well as a much larger range than the average CD store and the attraction of instant gratification, the iTunes store provides a price advantage. Not only are complete albums a little cheaper, but more importantly, you can buy single songs for not very much money at all. Buying that top 40 hit no longer requires you to pay for album filler material. The great attraction of the iTunes model is that spur-of-the-moment purchase of a single song from long ago, just remembered.

It's here that the cost equation of the Sony Portable Reader stumbles in comparison to the iPod model. The Reader can't utilise your existing library of books. There's currently no easy way to scan your current collection into a suitable electronic format. And forget about downloading content. Whilst Project Gutenberg and the like provide a wealth of public domain material, the stuff you want to read won't be there. The repository of free book downloads is dwarfed by that of free music (and in any case, specific downloads may not be readable by the Sony device).

Then there's Sony's pricing model on its own Connect store. It's not particularly attractive. At the time of writing, *Freakonomics* was selling as an ebook for US$15.96. On Amazon it was available for US$16.77 as a hardcover or US$10.99 as rough cut paperback. So, rather than paying less for a virtual book, Sony (and its partner publishers) is *expecting people to pay more*. Those publishers might argue that the ebook is cheaper than the recommended retail price (which for *Freakonomics* is $25.95) but online shoppers are perhaps more savvy that their bricks and mortar counterparts. And whilst a devoted reader might pay a few extra dollars to support their local independent bookshop, it's unlikely they'd want to do the same for a partnership between two multinational, multimedia global conglomerates. Especially for something they can't hold in their hands. It's also likely that readers understand that the costs of producing and distributing an ebook title are miniscule compared to the print version; their expectation is that there should be a significant price advantage over the bookshop price. Or at least enough to offset the purchase price of the Reader over a reasonable amount of time.

Adding to the problem is that the Connect store currently has little range to speak of. According to Sony, 10 000 titles are available. Which is comparable to a very modestly stocked small bookstore. A quick check showed that of Bill Bryson's 14 published books, four were available on the Connect store. Peter Carey's Booker Prize winners were not available nor was the 2006 Pulitzer Prize winner, Geraldine Brooks's *March*. As with pricing, the virtual bookshop has to do more than match the real one; it has to beat its range by a sizeable margin. The expectation for the digital library is much higher than a real-world bookshop, which even now might carry 20 times as many titles as Sony's Connect. The iTunes store has four million songs and there are still some glaring holes in its catalogue. Until the Connect store is comparable, the Reader ecosystem will not be taken seriously.

So, the Sony Portable Reader is no panacea in terms of commercial book publishing. Its screen technology is not yet perfect, its content provision is flawed. But it does represent further baby steps towards a future for book culture. What the Sony Reader suggests is that killing the object is becoming viable. It remains to be seen whether any single e-reading device will do for books what the iPod did for music (and the Reader is not as viscerally attractive as an iPod), but the device itself suggests that an acceptable, affordable reading apparatus is within our grasp. Reinforcing this impression, the Sony device is soon to be joined by cheaper alternatives from the likes of Amazon. All suggesting that this could be the first step in the journey of a thousand.

But a new reading device is only a *technical* step. What's needed is a *cultural* step. Publishers should build on such devices and make a return to a book culture; they should grasp the opportunity to reinvent book publishing entirely and build a heavenly library.

▶▶ CHAPTER 8.
The heavenly library

Any science or technology which is sufficiently advanced is indistinguishable from magic.

Arthur C Clarke[1]

Any technology distinguishable from magic is insufficiently advanced.

Barry Gehm[2]

It is late and we've all had a bit to drink, which probably explains the music that's playing; a medley of trashy hits from the '70s and '80s, songs that conjure up memories of a younger us. 'Do you have a copy of *Life on Mars*?' somebody asks. 'Not yet' I say, and hop online. A minute (and a dollar) later and it's playing in the dining room, provoking spontaneous singalongs and misty-eyed reminiscing. Magic.

The future didn't happen overnight, but its direction became clear around the time of the Napster lawsuit at the turn of the century. Before then, the idea that information could be unbound from objects was the stuff of techno-pundits who didn't live in the real world.[3] The spontaneous eruption of music-sharing changed everything; it was suddenly apparent to the rest of us that music didn't need be shipped around the planet on shiny plastic discs. And given that all information products could be digitised with relative ease, nor did anything else have to exist in physical form. Edgar Bronfman Jr (then head of Universal Music) summed it up with the vision: 'a few clicks of your mouse will make it possible for you to summon every book ever written in any language, every movie ever made, every television show ever produced, and every piece of music ever recorded'.[4]

Of course, the realisation of technical possibility is never simple. Cultural habits, legal hurdles, institutional inertia and economic constraints complicate and confuse. Despite these difficulties, the heavenly jukebox is pretty much here; it might be a few more years before all the world's music is available, but it's not far off. And it has opened up new ways of not just listening to, but finding music. Users get suggestions based on music that is already in their collection, or based on the samples they are listening to at the time. They get recommendations from peers, strangers and musicians. They get links to tracks that other people have bought. And they don't get dirty fingers from flipping through racks of plastic covers complete with misplaced discs, and incomplete collections.

I'll be honest, having browsed and bought online, the very idea of a CD shop fills me with dread; a feeling which I'm sharing with more and more people. In the US at the time of writing, Apple's online iTunes store was the fourth biggest music retailer in that country.[5] At the same time, Tower Records, an object-selling institution of a bygone age, shut up shop.[6] What happened first with music is spreading to other media forms. Television shows and movies are becoming available on the heavenly jukebox. You can legally download television from reality shows to soap operas, to classic episodes of *Nightrider*; and the first steps have been taken in the long march towards online distribution of Hollywood movies. Even the next-generation gaming consoles let you select from an online library of videogames, for a fee. Surely books, in a heavenly library, can't be far behind.

We can imagine the *heavenly library* as the world's collection of books available in an instant. It will be searchable, downloadable, readable with recommendations and suggestions from other readers, authors and critics; and a place to contribute to discussions about the book in question. Imagine that it will allow access to titles that might not be feasible in print (one in which *all* the Vogel shortlisters are published, not just the winner);[7] where the new Patrick Whites get to hang out their talent for as many books as is required to find their voice. Imagine a catalogue of niches, made possible and searchable via electronic delivery; enabling a different set of publishing economics and priorities.

The heavenly library could usher in an entirely new book ecosystem in which ideas are more important than objects; one in which reviews and critics can link directly to the book in question and conversation is encouraged, not stifled by the disconnection of print. Imagine a library in which entire backlists are instantly available and there is no such thing as 'out of print'; where almost any book can be found and where intelligent search locates titles that even the most knowledgeable sales assistant has never heard of. Anyone who has bought a book from Amazon or a song from iTunes knows what I'm talking about. Now instead of waiting for the book to ship from Amazon's warehouses or affiliates, imagine that your purchased book appears instantly on your computer or reading device.

Then imagine having all your books on a single device the size of a paperback; having the ability to search through your entire library in an instant and taking every Wilbur Smith novel ever published with you on your Fiji holiday. If it can happen with music (and it has), it should be able to happen with books.

And it would allow books the luxury of time. At the moment, publishers and booksellers gamble on how long to keep a book available to the general public. With the heavenly library, there is no gambling involved. Everything is always available; increasing the possibility that writers whose sales had been dormant for years might benefit from a revival.

▶▶ Finding readers

The heavenly library would solve problems for publishers too. Books seldom sell because of serendipitous discovery in a bookshop shelf. For the most part, they sell because people have heard about them; they have been recommended by friends or reviewed in the wider media. They have gained attention because they have won awards; or they have managed to draw attention to themselves via some clever marketing and packaging. A prominent display in a bookshop no doubt helps.

Publishers guess which titles to push; bookshops guess how many to stock, and cartons of books get shipped around at great expense so that a book can sit hopefully on a shelf somewhere. What's more, it might sit on the wrong shelf. Physical objects can only be in one place at a time, which is pretty inconvenient when it comes to stocking and displaying books. Apart from would-be-purchasers not putting the book back in the right place, there is the problem of categorisation. Is *Harry Potter* a children's book, or should it be in the fantasy section? Is *The Name of the Rose* crime or literature? Of course, if you order many copies, you could have some in each section but that doesn't work for all titles; and makes for a re-stocking nightmare.

Obscurity is the author's (and the publisher's) enemy and the easiest way to disappear is as one of thousands of books lining the shelves in a suburban megabookshop. Actually, there is one easier way to be invisible: and that's by not even making it to those shelves. Physical objects take up space, and even the biggest bookshops cannot stock everything. So, if the niche that you're appealing to is too small, your book won't just be obscure, in many bookshops, it will simply not exist.

Do it electronically and it all changes. Digital books can appear in any number of categories; they don't need to be shipped around the countryside in some mad game of readership roulette; and recommendations and reviews can sit where they're most useful: next to the books themselves.

And I don't buy the arguments of some, that there are already too many books. Mexican writer Gabriel Zaid might be correct when he says that it would take us 15 years just to read the list of all the books ever published,[8] but many of those are (as suggested previously) anti-books and functional books. What's more, many are out of print, and difficult to track down. Not that the heavenly library would necessarily result in more books being published. Instead, the reconfigured economies that it enables might mean that different books will be published. It's impossible to nominate titles that don't exist; but it might be easier to reflect on what constituted midlist titles in the past and consider whether they'd get a run in the current economic climate. We have seen how some books, now considered classics, had very low initial print runs, and would now not be considered worthy of publication. We have also seen that authors like VS Naipaul would, if starting out today, not be published. With the heavenly library, the dollar amounts are different, and the numbers required to justify publication should be much lower. Who knows how many contemporary Naipauls might be unearthed?

So the argument has to be one of institutional change. For example publishers could more feasibly experiment. Michael Heyward from Text Publishing argues that in Australia at least, not enough is published, and that it would be terrific to be able to publish more titles and let buyers decide on the worth of each publication.[9] The heavenly library would understand that books are niche products; not every book published needs to be read by everybody. Rather, a book merely needs to find its audience, which without the dead weight of object economics can be quite small. What's more, the heavenly library's reach would be international. All of a sudden, a novel which might sell a few copies to a particular inner-city set, could sell many times that number to the various inner-city sets around the planet. (Arguably, residents of Darlinghurst in inner Sydney have more in common with residents of the East Village than they do with the outer-Sydney suburb of Bella Vista.)

Selling books is about connecting readers and writers within a niche; something that is very hard when distributing atoms, but very easy when distributing bits. In *The Long Tail*, Chris Anderson suggests that the average book in the United States sells 500 copies.[10] In the print environment, connecting those 500 copies with the 500 people who wish to buy them is an incredible exercise in guesswork and logistics. There may be a few thousand people who want to read this book, but it's unlikely that they can be easily found by throwing some copies in each of a hundred bookshops. It would be far more effective to locate an appropriate 'community of interest' and distribute that way. The internet allows us to find that community globally rather than locally. Rather than guessing how many copies of a book should go to the local independent bookshop, it can be marketed to the appropriate interest group on the network.

What's more, a properly constructed heavenly library would know what readers' interests were, and provide suggestions and information about new titles. The mythical bookseller was one who knew their customer, and could suggest books they might enjoy. The heavenly library makes this possible; the library would have knowledge of previous purchases, and sufficient smarts about all of its new and existing titles to find appropriate suggestions. The technology is not new; it already works remarkably well with amazon.com.

▶▶│ Freeing publishers

As I suggested in Chapter 6, most books are already written on computers.[11] The files are sent electronically to a publisher, who finalises its contents, before it is turned into an appropriate format for pre-press and printing. During all of these electronic phases, the book still exists in its entirety. It has its 'edges defined', its ideas finalised, its time invested, all in electronic form. It can be read, dissected, analysed and discussed without ever having been printed. And this publishing process has happened to any good book long before ink hits paper and paper is bound.

There is absolutely no *technical* reason why an electronic version of the book cannot be distributed to readers; no *technical* reason why the workflow cannot be interrupted before printing, and no *technical* reason why the technologies of the internet can't be leveraged for immediate distribution. In short, apart from the still-evolving quality of a portable reading device, there is no *technical* reason why the heavenly library does not exist.

But the heavenly library is not so much a technical shift as a cultural one; demanding change in readers, writers and publishers. Such a displacement cannot happen easily, and may not occur until generational change is in place. But unless cultural change does take place, the culture will die.

Part of the cultural shift is a reinvention of the economics of book publishing; an acceptance that the heavenly library is a way out of the bind that prevents publishers from publishing books they love, because they won't make money. I'm not privy to the intricacies of the costs involved in running a publishing company, but instinct suggests that the heavenly library may redress that balance between commerce and culture.

With ebooks, publishing costs change significantly. Not only does that vast printing budget largely disappear, but so do warehousing and distribution costs. Now backlists can be held at almost no cost and all those courier charges for small bookshop orders are a thing of the past. With printed objects, the cost of books was largely about the cost of printing and selling. With electronic books, the real cost of books is largely the cost of writing and editing. So marginal books can be published, and publishers can focus on editorial, text design and marketing functions rather than printing and shipping.

You might remember the Australian publishing example I used in Chapter 5. If we assume that bookshop margins and printing and distribution costs disappear, we are left with fixed costs of $6500 plus an author royalty of $1.56 per copy sold. Let's speculate on an ebook, available online for a much lower retail price.

Table 8.1: Ebook profit potential

ebooks sold	RRP	income	royalty + costs	profit
3 000	$10	$30 000	$11 180	$18 820
3 000	$5	$15 000	$11 180	$3 820
1 500	$5	-$7 500	$8 840	-$1 340

Again, specific numbers can be massaged to suit any particular argument, but it seems entirely possible to price an ebook far more attractively than a printed book and still make a profit. Remember that ebooks have no warehousing cost and there is no risk of return; once the appropriate systems are in place, it's simply a matter of making the file available.

The heavenly library would also allow a shift in sales and marketing strategies. The internet has proven remarkably effective at connecting niches; and drawing people of similar interest together over time and space. Instead of relying on traditional localised mechanisms of distribution, publicity, sales and marketing, the virtual object of the ebook can travel as easily to Istanbul as it can to Invercargill. If the marketing for a title is done properly – and globally – then the target market for an ebook is potentially far greater than for its print equivalent.

▶▶❙ Tactility or the planet?

But many will mourn the loss of the object; the physical feeling of a well-thumbed book and the touch of finely printed paper. And some of them will not be convinced that losing the object will result in a reinvigorated book culture. To the unswerving, I offer one more reason for the heavenly library. A less-discussed benefit of the shift to the virtual is an environmental one. A dead-tree book is just that. A dead tree. But the environmental impact of the printed object goes beyond the mere absence of another tree. Not only are books printed on paper, but they are shipped, sometimes halfway around the world. By the time it reaches its reader, the average paperback has cost the equivalent of three kilograms (over 6.6 pounds) of carbon dioxide emissions. Then add in the industry's sale or return policies, and a substantial proportion of those paperbacks are then *shipped back* to the publisher, who might warehouse them. Or pulp them. Dave Reay, author of *Climate Change Begins at Home*, suggests that every year, the UK publishing industry 'in effect, puts an extra 100000 cars on the road'.[12]

The heavenly library would, in theory, have a significant impact on that figure. And before naysayers suggest that the production of an electronic reading device would itself result in significant carbon emissions, the manufacturer's figures suggest otherwise. Matsushita claim that their reader produces the emissions of 14 book equivalents in its production.[13] So, after buying a dozen books or so in ebook form, the planet is ahead.

▶▶| Hurdles and hoops

Of course, problems must be overcome and issues need to be addressed. But working through change is necessary in every industry. The car required an enormous amount of infrastructure – from roads through petrol stations – that took decades to properly emerge. And telephones were pretty well useless until enough people actually possessed them and network effects could kick in. As the opportunities of the new media technologies emerge, the sceptics will place hurdles in the pathway of possible change and argue that because of those hurdles, change is impossible. But other media industries *are* adapting to the new media environment. The challenge in that change is to preserve the qualities that make a medium unique. With books, killing the object is the only way to preserve the unique qualities of book culture; change is not only welcome but necessary. Otherwise, book culture will disappear.

But the problem of standards needs to be addressed. Not moral and ethical standards, nor quality standards (although they are all worth thinking about). No, one key hurdle blocking the heavenly library is an appropriate technical standard. Sony's Reader uses a proprietary file format, Adobe and Microsoft have their own prejudices and the übergeeks argue for 'openness' with almost religious fervour.[14] Think 'Beta vs VHS' or 'Windows vs Macintosh' and you get the idea. I don't have any immediate solutions, but the most pragmatic approach for publishers would be to ensure that the chosen file format can be transcoded easily into any other. That way, the ebook can follow the market. Lessons can be drawn from music: there are many competing formats for selling music online, but the record companies seem to have little difficulty in providing files in whatever format is required.

Tied in with a file format standard is the issue of copyright. In fact, with other media forms, the loudest arguments have been about how to prevent people from 'stealing' music or films. Publishers are keen to protect their assets, and will probably insist that electronic books have some kind of digital rights management (DRM) built into their formats, thus preventing 'illegitimate' copying. The problem is that such systems are contentious and tend to lock-in users to a particular technological approach. In the music realm, Apple appears to have found the appropriate copyright balance with the iPod and the iTunes store: users can play their music on a number of devices, but the DRM software prevents easy widespread copying. Book publishers need to find a similar balance. An added hurdle is that book publishing history is tied up in national boundaries, rights and copyright laws that speak to a nineteenth-century mindset, and set up barriers to access. These must be overcome if the heavenly library is to be realised.

There is also a workflow issue.[15] Whilst creating an electronic copy is easy *in theory*, it is often more difficult in practice because publishing workflows are still directed towards the printed object. Last-minute copy changes and editorial decisions are all predicated on the book as an object; so changes may occur, literally, at the press. However, as I've suggested, most of the book production workflow is digital and similar industries (such as newspapers) have managed to migrate to an online distribution strategy without significant drama. It's not too much to expect book publishers to be similarly successful in their migration.

Then, there is cost. Whilst the cost for new titles is (I would argue) negligible, the cost to digitise older books is quite high if digital versions do not exist. Scanning print copies is labour intensive, and the vast catalogue of a publishers' backlist suggests that much work is required. Luckily, there are companies offering to do it for free. The Google Book Search project,[16] for example, plans to digitise all books for no cost. For some mad reason, rather than take advantage of this largesse, publishers are resisting. Instead of seeing the Google project as a way to begin building the heavenly library, the book trade has, for the most part, circled its wagons, in the hope that the marauding hordes will just go away. But they won't. As the music industry knows, tradition means nothing to a newly empowered generation; more and more they see the heavenly library as a birthright.

Finally, there is the question of bookshops; if the heavenly library were to become a reality, then surely their role would be diminished. Perhaps, but their role is already diminished. Bookshops would still sell books that do need printing; illustrated books, gift books and blockbusters for casual readers. What they won't do is hold shelves of stock. Instead, they could sell a range of reading devices, and provide access points for the heavenly library. For those who prefer paper, they could sell print-on-demand services. The best ookshops provide a social space where book culture can occur; with author events, discussions and bookclub resources. Without bookshelves taking up valuable real estate, more energy could be devoted to that aspect of the business.

▶▶   A modest proposal

I began this book with a search for definitions and ended up with the notion that books are *machines for reading*. Books require time to cultivate and communicate ideas, and to converse about those ideas. Book culture springs from being able to – slowly – reflect and engage in the human conversation as both a reader and a writer. The reading machine requires readers, writers and publishers, and means by which writers can write, publishers can publish and readers can read. Over the last 20 years, writing and publishing has migrated to the digital realm; and if book culture is to have a future, reading must too.

I am not alone in this vision, if I were, then the book would have no future. For example, Jason Epstein sees Google Book Search as a project which is 'raising the theoretical possibility that every book ever printed in whatever language may indeed be accessed wherever Internet connections exist'.[17] Where Epstein and I differ is in the need for the printed object. His reading solution is print-on-demand; a series of kiosks which create finished books from the vast database of the heavenly library. I don't believe that final step is necessary, but even if he is right, publishing needs to shift its focus away from the object and onto its contents.

And it can begin with a few simple steps. Firstly, publishers need to make their entire catalogue of titles available digitally for a reasonable fee. Granted, this isn't going to happen overnight, but a constant drip feed of ebook releases would get the process in motion. Choice of format, digital rights management and cost are non-trivial decisions that each publisher would have to consider. If it were me, I'd build an online store that sold files in Adobe's pdf format (sized appropriately for the most popular e-reading devices) with no DRM, and charge enough to maintain margins and author royalties. But that's just me.

And I'd begin with a mix of backlist titles and bestsellers to get the show on the road. Content lessons can be drawn from the music industry. Not only do the most successful online stores have the largest catalogues of music, but publishers are now exploring the new economies of the *objectless* sale. Universal Music in Europe has recently created a *download-only* back catalogue, which currently consists of 3000 tracks stretching back several decades. There is no CD version of the music in question, it is only available as a digital download from an internet service such as iTunes. So far, a quarter of a million tracks have been sold, which considering the minimal cost of reissuing the music, seems to be a step in the right direction. By forgoing the object, Universal eventually hopes to reinstate over 100 000 previously deleted recordings.[18]

Secondly, publishers should establish ebook only lists, targeting specific reading niches. Again, this would mirror the music industry where Warner's Cordless and Universal's UMe labels[19] are download-only catalogues focusing on new releases from smaller bands. According to its press release, Cordless is a

> community intended to give new artists their chance, and a process that connects an audience to our artists' creativity …
> In addition to promoting its artists through online and offline marketing, traditional and lifestyle marketing, touring and radio promotion, Cordless artists' music will also be available on a variety of online music services.[20]

It seems like a useful model from which book publishers might borrow, and would be a useful experiment in ebook publishing. Academic publishers are already exploring this process. As well as the shift of journals into the online space, some publishers such as Melbourne University Press have an ebook list which allows readers to purchase titles in electronic form.

Science-fiction might also be a good place to start. Many sci-fi authors and publishers already have a big ebook presence, with some such as Baen Books *giving away* vast selections from their catalogue in a number of digital formats. It's interesting that anecdotal evidence suggests that, for now, giving away free ebooks is a good way of boosting sales of printed books. Eric Flint, from Baen writes:

> After all, Dave Weber's *On Basilisk Station* has been available for free as a 'loss leader' for Baen's for-pay experiment 'Webscriptions' for months now. And – hey, whaddaya know? – over that time it's become Baen's most popular backlist title in paper![21]

Thirdly, publishers need to think carefully about how they use the new media technologies. If books are to remain a key part of our culture's conversation, then they should create places where we can talk about books. Writers' festivals are useful, but highly localised and last about four days, every 12 months or so. Their presence could be complemented by a much more visible online book culture, where readers, writers and publishers can meet *virtually* anytime and anyplace. By creating these social networks, individual booklovers congregate and become something resembling a community, a place where book culture can thrive.

Finally, publishers should seek partnerships that have the potential to expand book culture; that is increase readership of *real* books, provoke discussion about reading and writing and generally continue the greater human conversation. These include *partnering* with established online vendors such as Amazon and Google to ensure that their ebooks can be found easily online. Co-operating with device manufacturers is also key; to ensure that the new economics of ebook publishing work for users, and to develop financial tools which would cushion the cost of the reading apparatus. Just as mobile telephony networks subsidise the cost of telephone handsets, publishers need to explore similar models. Getting a free Sony Reader if you commit to buying an ebook a week over a year sounds like a pretty good deal to me. Publishers might also want to explore subscription models, in which readers can download and read 'all-you-can-eat' style for a monthly fee.

None of these steps are guaranteed to result in a particular outcome. What they suggest are mechanisms that could again privilege book culture over commerce, without jeopardising the business that is books. For the immediate future, the printed book will probably work better for casual readers and blockbuster titles. Not everybody wants to invest in an electronic reader for that one book read over the summer vacation. But for serious reading, and serious readers, the heavenly library would make every niche viable and connect readers and writers more effectively than ever.

▶▶   The book is dead. Long live the book

Debates about the future of books are filled with red herrings. So, let's be clear about a few things. Books as objects will not disappear overnight as new media forms tend to *displace* rather than *replace* older ones. So, printed books will be around for some time to come. But despite the size of the 'book-object' industry, it doesn't have much room for book culture. Reading – the sort of reading that demands time, concentration and rewards readers for their commitment and willingness to immerse themselves in the text – is a niche activity. More people watch *Desperate Housewives* than curl up with a novel, any novel. *Grand Theft Auto* is now the target of moral panic that was once the domain of *Lady Chatterley* and MySpace gobbles up content and spits it out faster than a politician can jump to conclusions. At a time of instant gratification and immediate communication, selling 'reading' books is not the most profitable of activities. Some titles might emerge as blockbusters, but the majority will struggle to find their niche. The difficulty of physically linking readers to books dooms books to obscurity.

The print book industry is not motivated by book culture; books are largely published solely because they will sell *now*. The dependency on printing, with its physical and economic constraints means that the book trade emphasises objects over ideas; return on investment over notions of culture. The role that books once played in the human conversation (maybe because they were once *the only means* of conducting that conversation) is no longer a priority. The whole shebang still works as a money-making enterprise. There might still be enough interest in a few blockbuster titles to keep the dead-tree thing afloat, but it exists for different reasons. For those who care about book culture, it's all over. For *readers and authors*, the book is dead. But the heavenly library offers hope.

The new technologies are not a threat, but an opportunity. The internet is not a *thing*, but an *enabler*. It is a network which connects people and information and in doing so provokes a number of social and cultural effects. Its ubiquity and openness makes the invisible visible; its reach and accessibility mean it acts as an amplifier which increases the volume of an information event, and the speed at which it propagates (as well as the speed with which it becomes irrelevant). The internet does not replace any media form (be it audio, video or text). But it can act as a mechanism for distribution and promotion, a venue for entertainment, a space for conversation. The internet does not do what books do, it is where the book can be reinvigorated.

The future of the book need not reside in experimental works – networked books, liquid versions or hypertextual virtualities – although some of those ideas offer interesting possibilities. Rather, the immediate future of the book can be assured (long live the book) by disconnecting the ideas from the object, removing the physical constraints of dead trees and building a future without the codex. E-reading devices have so far been imperfect, but experience (and Moore's Law)[22] suggest that stasis is not permanent. It's not the technical step, but the required cultural step that is likely to prove most difficult to take.

Compared to cultural change, building a convincing e-reading device is a cinch. Constructing an ecosystem that speaks to book culture will prove far more difficult than producing a readable electronic screen. It's not something that will happen overnight. But for those who love reading, it may be the only way out.

I wrote this book because I love books, and want a future in which reading still happens, and books still matter, at least to some of us. Alan Kay, a pioneer of the computer age, once said that the 'best way to predict the future is to invent it'.[23] I'm no engineer, so building the hardware is not something I can do. But we can build the culture by having a conversation about the book and its future. This book is a provocation; its aim is to get that conversation going. Hopefully it will continue at www. thebookisdead.com. See you there.

▶▶| Notes

Website addresses have a habit of changing, so in order to keep these endnotes useful we've directed you to search the home page of most websites cited. Full addresses can be found at <http://www.thebookisdead.com>. All websites in this notes section were accessed in February 2007.

▶▶| PROLOGUE

1   John Browning (1993) 'Libraries without Walls for Books without Pages', *Wired*, 'Issue 1.01', search <http://www.wired.com>.
2   Alan Lightman (1993) *Einstein's Dreams*, Pantheon Books, New York, search <http://www.amazon.com>.

▶▶| CHAPTER 1. The book is dead

1   Kevin Kelly (2006) 'Scan this Book!', *New York Times Magazine*, 14 May, search <http://www.nytimes.com>.
2   John Updike gave a speech to BookExpo America 2006 in response to Kevin Kelly's article. Bob Thompson (2006) 'Explosive Words', *Washington Post*, 22 May, search <http://www.washingtonpost.com>.
3   Laura J Miller (2006) *Reluctant Capitalists; Bookselling and the Culture of Consumption*, University of Chicago Press, Chicago.
4   Marshall McLuhan (1962) *The Gutenberg Galaxy*, University of Toronto Press, Toronto.
5   See, for example John B Thompson (1995) *Media and Modernity*, Polity Press, Cambridge.
6   DD McNicoll (2006) 'Hard Fact on Book Sales Sells Good Fiction Short', *Australian*, 22 July.
7   Tom Dyckhoff (2001) 'They've Got it Covered', *Guardian*, 15 September, search <http://books.guardian.co.uk>.
8   Chris Anderson (2005) *The Long Tail*, Random House Business Books, London, p 121.
9   Search Random House <http://www.randomhouse.com> for 'Stephen Hawking'.
10 Search Internet Movie Database <http://imdb.com> for '*Metropolitan*' by Whit Stillman.
11 National Endowment for the Arts (2004) 'Reading at Risk: A Survey of Literary Reading in America', National Endowment for the Arts, Washington DC.
12 The book is *The Last Juror* by John Grisham. Complete sales data from

the Australian Publishers Association (2006) '2005 Bestsellers Survey', available from <http://www.publishers.asn.au> click on 'Industry statistics' and 'Bestsellers survey'.

13 The average attendance for 2005 AFL games at the MCG was 40813. The highest was Carlton v Collingwood when over 60000 attended. The lowest was Carlton v Fremantle with 16000: see <http://www.mcg.org.au> click on 'MCG Attendances', '2005 AFL Season'.

14 A typical number one show according to Oztam figures (which manages and markets ratings) draws over two million viewers. For the week ending 29 September 2006, the number 10 show was *Australian Idol* which drew 1.5 million viewers. See <http://www.oztam.com.au> for weekly Australian TV ratings data.

15 The comparison was made at the 2blowhards blog, search <http://www.2blowhards.com>.

16 John Sutherland (2006) *How to Read a Novel*, Profile Books, London, pp 34–36.

17 This honour was bestowed by Agnes Hooper Gottlieb, Henry Gottlieb, Barbara Bowers and Brent Bowers (1998) *1000 Years, 1000 People: Ranking the Men and Women who Shaped the Millennium*, Kodansha America, New York.

18 Economist (1999) 'Talking to the World: Millennium Issue: Communication', *Economist*, 23 December, search <http://economist.com>.

19 John Naughton (2006) 'Websites that Changed the World', *Observer*, 13 August, search <http://observer.guardian.co.uk>.

20 Shelton Gunaratne (2001) 'Paper, Printing and the Printing Press, A Horizontally Integrative Macrohistory Analysis', *Gazette*, vol 63 (6), pp 459–479.

21 'Just One Book', discussion post on *The Thorn Tree*, Lonely Planet, search <http://thorntree.lonelyplanet.com>.

22 'Seeking a Good EBook Reading Device', search *Slashdot* <http://ask.slashdot.org>.

23 Pierre Bourdieu argues that 'the fundamental methodological problem for all social inquiry is the construction of the object'. See Jonathan Sterne (1999) 'Thinking the Internet', in Steve Jones (ed) *Doing Internet Research*, Sage, Thousand Oaks.

▶▶ CHAPTER 2. What is a book?

1 Gilles Deleuze and Felix Guattari (1987) *A Thousand Plateaus* (B Massumi Trans), University of Minnesota Press, Minneapolis, p 407.

2 Jason Epstein (2001) *Book Business*, WW Norton, New York, p 86.

3 Elizabeth Eisenstein (1997) *The Printing Press as an Agent of Change*, Cambridge University Press, Cambridge.

4 Walter Ong (1988) *Orality & Literacy: The Technologizing of the Word*, Methuen, New York.

5 Marshall McLuhan (1962) *The Gutenberg Galaxy*, University of Toronto Press, Toronto.

6 Neil Postman (1986) *Amusing Ourselves to Death*, Penguin, New York.

7 McLuhan op cit.

8   Malcolm Knox (2005) 'The Rise of Bookscan', *Monthly*, May, Issue 1.

9   My partner worked as a book rep for years, and every month she would come home with a stack of covers and blurbs, which she would place in a folder and take to bookshops to entice.

10   I had lunch with a publishing friend recently, who lamented that her days were spent 'sucking up to key account reps'.

11   Nick Hornby (2004) *The Polysyllabic Spree*, McSweeneys, San Francisco, p 125.

12   Sven Birkerts (1994) *The Gutenberg Elegies*, Fawcett, Columbine.

13   PJ O'Rourke's springboard was a *National Lampoon* article, appearing in March of 1979, 'How to Drive Fast on Drugs While Getting Your Wing-Wang Squeezed and Not Spill Your Drink'. It later appeared in his first book, *Republican Party Reptile* (1987) Atlantic Monthly Pr, New York.

14   Jason Epstein (2001) *Book Business*, WW Norton, New York; André Schiffrin (2000) *The Business of Books*, Verso, London.

15   Melvyn Bragg (2006) *Twelve Books that Changed the World*, Hodder & Stoughton, London: *Principia Mathematica* by Isaac Newton (1687); *Married Love* by Marie Stopes (1918); *Magna Carta* by Members of the English Ruling Classes (1215); *The Rule Book of Association Football* by a Group of Former English Public School Men (1863); *On the Origin of Species* by Charles Darwin (1859); *On the Abolition of the Slave Trade* by William Wilberforce in Parliament, immediately printed in several versions (1789); *A Vindication of the Rights of Woman* by Mary Wollstonecraft (1792); *Experimental Researches in Electricity* by Michael Faraday (3 volumes, 1839, 1844, 1855); *Patent Specification for Arkwright's Spinning Machine* by Richard Arkwright (1769); *The King James Bible* translation by William Tyndale and 54 Scholars Appointed by the King (1611); *An Inquiry into the Nature and Causes of the Wealth of Nations* by Adam Smith (1776); *The First Folio* by William Shakespeare (1623). Search <http://books.guardian.co.uk>.

16   Jeff Martin (2005) 'Voyager Company CD-ROMs: Production History and Preservation Challenges of Commercial Interactive Media' <http://resourceguide.eai.org/preservation/computer/pdf-docs/voyager_casestudy.pdf>.

17   Birkerts op cit p 162.

18   Louise Williams (2006) 'No More Pencils, No More Books', *Sydney Morning Herald*, 5 April, search <http://smh.com.au>.

19   Tim Berners-Lee (1999) *Weaving the Web*, Orion Business, London. For his role in the creation of the world wide web see Chapter 4.

20   Jürgen Habermas (1991) *The Structural Transformation of the Public Sphere*, MIT Press, Cambridge.

21   James Gleick (1999) *Faster*, Abacus, London, pp 171–172. See also <http://fasterbook.com>.

22   Benedict Anderson (1991) *Imagined Communities*, Verso, London, revised edition.

23   Douglas Adams (1999) 'How to Stop Worrying and Learn to Love the Internet', *Sunday Times*, 29 August, search <http://www.douglasadams.com>.

24   Bill Cope and Angus Phillips (2006) *The Future of the Book in the Digital*

Age, Chandos Publishing, Oxford, pp 7–8.

25   Howard Kurtz (2006) 'The Latest Chapters on the War', *Washington Post*, 16 October, C01.

26   John Carey (2005) *What Good are the Arts?*, Faber and Faber, London, p 214.

▶▌   CHAPTER 3. Nobody reads

1   Philip Roth cited in Esther B Fein (1993) 'Philip Roth Sees Double. And Maybe Tripe, Too', *New York Times*, 9 March, search <http://www.nytimes.com>.

2   National Endowment for the Arts (2004) 'Reading at Risk: A Survey of Literary Reading', National Endowment for the Arts, Washington DC.

3   W McLennan (1997) 'Cultural Trends in Australia: A Statistical Overview 1997', ABS Catalogue No 4172.0, Australian Bureau of Statistics, Canberra, p 17.

4   Steven Roger Fischer (2003) *A History of Reading*, Reaktion Books, London, p 263.

5   Alberto Manguel (1996) *A History of Reading*, Penguin, London.

6   Nick Hornby (2004) *The Polysyllabic Spree*, McSweeneys, San Francisco, p 58.

7   Zadie Smith (2006) quoted in 'Zadie Smith and the Practice of Reading', *Boing Boing*, search <http://www.boingboing.net>.

8   Sven Birkerts (1994) *The Gutenberg Elegies*, Fawcett, Columbine, p 32.

9   John Carey (2005) *What Good are the Arts?*, Faber and Faber, London, p 208.

10   James Bradley (2006) 'The Fuss over Super-fine Fiction', *Australian*, 7 November, search <http://www.theaustralian.news.com.au>.

11   John Freeman (2005) 'Why Fiction is a Phoenix', *Australian*, 24 December, search <http://www.theaustralian.news.com.au>.

12   ibid p 3.

13   Nielsen Bookscan (2004) *Book Sales Yearbook 2003*, Book 2 'The Year in Detail: Subjects, Books, Authors', Bookseller Publications, London.

14   Carmen Lawrence (2007) 'The Reading Sickness', *Journal of the Association for the Study of Australian Literature*, vol 6, search <http://www.nla.gov.au>.

15   Ramona Koval (2004) 'Books and Writing – The Fate of Fiction', *ABC Radio National*, 28 November <http://www.abc.net.au/rn/arts/bwriting/stories/s1252776.htm>.

16   Allan Luke (1992) 'The Variability of Reading Practices' in Jock Macleod and Pat Buckridge (eds) *Books and Reading in Australian Society*, Institute for Cultural Policy Studies, Griffith University, Brisbane, p 122.

17   ibid p 121.

18   See Robert Darnton (1999) 'The New Age of the Book', *New York Review of Books*, vol 46, no 5, 18 March <http://www.nybooks.com/articles/546>. There are numerous examples of prize-winning academic books that sell fewer than 500 copies. For example, the best books in a series edited by Roy Rosenzweig at George Mason University sold 282 copies. Penn State University Press published a title on Islam in Central Asia that won four

awards, received terrific reviews and sold 215 copies in cloth (and 691 in hardback). Also, see John B Thompson (2005) *Books in the Digital Age*, Polity Press, Cambridge, pp 98–102.

19   Kimberly Maul (2006) 'Books a $35 Billion Industry, Reports BISG', *Book Standard*, 19 May; Book Industry Study Group (2006) 'Book Industry Trends 2006 Shows Publishers' Net Revenues at $34.59 Billion for 2005', BISG Press Release, 22 May <http://www.bisg.org/news/press.php?pressid=35>.

20   Australian Bureau of Statistics (2004) 'Book Publishers Australia 2003–04', search <http://www.abs.gov.au>.

21   AAP (2006) 'Australians Gambling $15.5 Billion a Year', *Sydney Morning Herald*, 20 September, search <http://www.smh.com.au>.

22   Australian Bureau of Statistics (2005) 'Book Publishers Australia, 2003–04', p 7, search <http://www.abs.gov.au>.

23   ibid p 16.

24   Gallup Poll (2005) 'About Half of Americans Reading a Book', 3 June, search <http://www.galluppoll.com>.

25   Barry Riley (Umina) (2006) 'Letters', *Sydney Morning Herald*, 14 September, search <http://www.smh.com.au>.

26   Jennifer Sexton (2006) 'Why Bother with Patrick White?', *Australian*, 15 July, search <http://www.theaustralian.news.com.au>.

27   I only recall one online analysis of Mark Latham's books, which seemed to be more concerned with his apparent inconsistencies than anything else: Chris Saliba (2004) 'The Dummies Guide to Mark Latham', *Crikey*, search <http://www.crikey.com.au>.

28   Neil Postman (1986) *Amusing Ourselves to Death*, Penguin, New York, p 34.

29   ibid p 35.

30   ibid.

31   Thomas Paine (1776) *Common Sense*, Great Books Online <http://www.bartleby.com/133>.

32   Joan Didion (2006) 'Cheney: The Fatal Touch', *New York Review of Books*, vol 53, no 15, 5 October <http://www.nybooks.com/articles/19376>.

33   Carey op cit p 209.

34   See NSW Premier's Reading Challenge <http://www.schools.nsw.edu.au/premiersreadingchallenge/rules.htm>.

35   William B Goodman (1983) 'Thinking about Readers', in Stephen Graubard (ed) *Reading in the 1980s*, RR Bowker, New York, pp 71–75.

36   ibid p 77.

37   Ian McEwan (2005) 'Hello, Would you Like a Free Book?', *Guardian*, 20 September, search <http://www.guardian.co.uk>.

38   Ian Watts (2000) *The Rise of the Novel*: Studies in Defoe, Richardson and Fielding, Pimlico, London, p 44.

39   Martyn Lyons (2003) 'New Readers in the Nineteenth Century', in Guglielmo Cavallo and Roger Chartier (eds) *A History of Reading in the West*, Polity, Cambridge, pp 316–319.

40   McEwan op cit.

41   Bill Gates (1996) 'Business @ the Speed of Thought', Microsoft, search <http://www.microsoft.com>.

42   Jakob Nielsen (1997) 'Concise, Scannable and Objective, How to Write for the Web', *Useit* <http://www.useit.com/papers/webwriting/writing. html>.

43   Keith Blanchard, quoted in Michael Scherer (2002) 'Magazine Writing: Does Size Matter?', *Columbia Journalism Review*, issue 6, November/ December <http://www.cjr.org/issues/2002/6/mag-scherer.asp>.

44   Needham, quoted in ibid.

45   Scherer op cit.

46   ibid.

47   John Birkenshaw (2006) 'The Future of Magazines and Direct Mail 2015– 2020: Implications for the Printing Industry', *Pira Consulting Report*, March, Pira International, prepared for British Printing Industries Federation, p 33 <http://www.britishprint.com/downloads/pira-report-low.pdf>.

48   Search New Yorker Store for *The Complete New Yorker* <http://www. thenewyorkerstore.com>.

49   *Washington City Paper* (2004) Department of Media, 1–7 October, cited in <http://crocolyle.blogspot.com/2004_10_03_crocolyle_archive.html>.

50   'The Future of Newspapers' (2006) *Independent*, 13 November <http:// news.independent.co.uk/media/article1963543.ece>.

51   Tim O'Reilly (2006) 'What Job does a Book do?', *O'Reilly Radar* <http:// radar.oreilly.com/archives/2006/04/what_job_does_a_book_do.html>.

52   A typical paperback in Australia costs $20–$30. A brand name 42 inch plasma television can be had for just under $2000.

53   John Sutherland (2006) *How to Read a Novel*, Profile Books, London, p 46.

54   Patrick Buckridge (2006) 'Readers and Reading', in Craig Munro and Robyn Sheahan-Bright (eds) (2006) *Paper Empires, A History of the Book in Australia 1946–2005*, University of Queensland Press, Brisbane.

55   Watts op cit p 42.

56   'The body' is reported to have once said that 'I never read anything I haven't written myself'. Macpherson has since recanted, and in an interview with *Easy Living Magazine* she said: 'I love Paul Auster and I'm reading *Hegemony Or Survival* by Noam Chomsky, which is really interesting. I read in bed and I read when I travel.' 17 February 2006. See <http://www. easylivingmagazine.com/RealLife/CelebrityInterview/ElleMacpherson/ default.aspx>.

▶▌   CHAPTER 4. Everybody writes

1   'Gore Vidal has remarked that there are no true readers today, only would- be writers. Everyone wants to write a novel: nobody wants to read one.' Cited in John Bayley (1999) 'Other Worlds to Inhabit' in Dale Salwak (1999) *A Passion for Books*, Macmillan, London, p 21.

2   Well over half the authors who have won Vogels have publications in the National Library. See Tess Brady (2006) 'Case study: *The Australian*/Vogel Literary Award', in Craig Munro and Robyn Sheahan-Bright (eds) (2006) *Paper Empires, a History of the Book in Australia 1946–2005*, University of Queensland Press, Brisbane.

3   Roland Barthes (1967) 'Death of the Author', *Aspen*, Fall–Winter, Roaring Fork Press, New York City <http://www.ubu.com/aspen/aspen5and6/

index.html>.

4   Lyn Tranter tells the story: 'Listen, I had a thing years ago with an author (who will remain nameless, of course) but her name started with a "W", and a large publishing company said they wanted to change it to start with a "D"', Ramona Koval (2005) 'Books and Writing – BookScan and the Fading Mystique of Literary Australia', *ABC Radio National*, 31 July <http://www.abc.net.au/rn/arts/bwriting/stories/s1425012.htm>.

5   David Free (2005) 'To get Published you have to be Famous First', *Sydney Morning Herald*, 23 September, search <http://www.smh.com.au>.

6   Tim Berners-Lee (1999) *Weaving the Web*, Orion Business, London, p 182.

7   Jon Casimir (2002) 'For the Love Of', Icon, *Sydney Morning Herald*, 1 November.

8   Jeanette Winterson discussed the reluctance of some authors to embrace the new media in a piece for the *Industry Standard*, which she reproduced on <http://www.jeanettewinterson.com/pages/content/index.asp?PageID=115>.

9   Darren Waters (2005) 'Pick of the Blogs: Boing Boing', 20 July, search <http://www.bbc.co.uk>.

10   'Book Lust: Sydney Writers' Festival 2006' (2006) *ABC Television*, 30 May.

11   Darren Rouse (2005) used Site Meter to survey a number of popular blogs. According to his stats the average reader spends 96 seconds reading the average blog. See 'How Long Do Your Readers Stay at Your Blog – Length of Stay Statistics', 17 March <http://www.problogger.net/archives/2005/03/17/how-long-do-your-readers-stay-at-your-blog-length-of-stay-statistics>.

12   Margot Kingston (2001) 'Web Diary Charter', 26 April, search <http://www.smh.com.au>. See also <http://webdiary.com.au/cms>.

13   The 2007 Lulu Blooker Prize <http://www.lulublookerprize.com/faq.php17>.

14   Janet Kornblum (2006) 'The Blooker Awards, For Books Arising from Blogs', *USA Today*, 2 April, search <http://www.usatoday.com>.

15   See for example, 'Publishers say Few Hits on Blog Books', *Librarians' Place*, search <http://librariansplace.wordpress.com>; John Scalzi (2006) 'The Old Media Toilers Help Themselves to a Heaping Slice of Schadenfreude Pie', *Whatever* <http://www.scalzi.com/whatever/004487.html>.

16   Jim Giles (2005) 'Internet Encyclopedias go Head to Head', *Nature*, vol 438, 15 December, search <http://www.nature.com>.

17   David Marshall and Robert Burnett (2003) *Web Theory*, Routledge, London, pp 126–152.

▶▌   CHAPTER 5. What do publishers do?

1   PJ O'Rourke (2005) 'Here's a Tax We Can All Agree On', 30 May, search <http://pjorourkeonline.blogspot.com>.

2   Bill Cope and Angus Phillips (2006) 'Introduction', *The Future of the Book in the Digital Age*, Chandos Publishing, Oxford, p 10.

3   ibid pp 8–9.

4   André Schiffrin (2000) *The Business of Books*, Verso, London, p 11.

5   Jason Epstein (2001) *Book Business*, WW Norton, New York, p 5.

6   Schiffrin op cit p 11.
7   ibid p 89.
8   ibid p 99.
9   ibid pp 110–111.
10 ibid pp 67–69.
11 Go to HarperCollins <http://b2b.harpercollins.co.uk> click on 'About HarperCollins' and 'History'.
12 Go to Simon & Schuster <http://www.simonsays.com> click on 'About Simon & Schuster' and 'Overview'.
13 Schiffrin op cit p 68.
14 The power of cross-media promotion shouldn't be underestimated. In the last decade, 19 of the top selling books were movie tie-ins. See Bob Minzesheimer (2004) '10 Years of Best Sellers: How the Book Landscape has Changed', *USA Today*, search <http://www.usatoday.com>.
15 Gayle Feldman (2005) 'Best and Worst of Times: The Changing Business of Trade Books, 1975–2002', National Arts Journalism Program, Columbia University, New York, p 4.
16 'Publishers Write off Winners' (2006) *Australian*, 2 January, search <http://www.theaustralian.news.com.au>.
17 Jennifer Sexton (2006) 'Why Bother with Patrick White?' *Australian*, 15 July, search <http://www.theaustralian.news.com.au>.
18 Matthew Kelly (2006) 'Books need Buyers', *Australian*, 4 October, search <http://www.theaustralian.news.com.au>.
19 Carmen Lawrence (2007) 'The Reading Sickness', *Journal of the Association for the Study of Australian Literature*, vol 6, search <http://www.nla.gov.au>.
20 Ed Pilkington (2006) 'Custom Outlets – US Publishing's New Holy Grail', *Guardian*, 4 November, search <http://books.guardian.co.uk>.
21 Julie Bosman (2006) 'Selling Literature to Go with Your Lifestyle', *New York Times*, search <http://www.nytimes.com>.
22 Feldman op cit p 4.
23 Frank Mott (1947) 'Golden Multitudes', cited in ibid p 15.
24 Feldman op cit p 16.
25 Gal Beckermann (2004) 'The Education of Stacy Sullivan', *Columbia Journalism Review*, September/October <http://www.cjr.org/issues/2004/5/ideas-books-beckerman.asp>.
26 David Kirkpatrick (2000) 'Report to the Authors Guild Midlist Books Study Committee', Authors Guild, p 25 <http://www.authorsguild.org/miscfiles/midlist.pdf>.
27 André Schiffrin (2000) *The Business of Books*, Verso, London, pp 109–110.
28 Anna Genoese (2006) 'Demystifying Publishing', *Live Journal* <http://alg.livejournal.com/84032.html>.
29 Denise Little (2001) 'The Profit Motive', *Bulletin of The Science Fiction and Fantasy Writers of America*, Fall, 2001 (151) <http://sfwa.org/bulletin/articles/profit-motive.html>.
30 Peter Dimock (no date), 'The Presence of Reading in Context', *Context: A Forum for Literary Arts and Culture*, no 2 <http://www.centerforbookculture.org/context/no2/dimock.html>.
31 Australian Bureau of Statistics (2005) 'Book Publishers Australia 1363.0',

Canberra, p 10.

▶▎ CHAPTER 6. Objects of desire

1   Cory Doctorow (2004) 'Ebooks: Neither E, Nor Books', Paper for the O'Reilly Emerging Technologies Conference <http://craphound.com/ebooksneitherenorbooks.txt>.

2   John Ezard (2005) 'One in Three has Bought a Book just to Look Intelligent', *Guardian*, 24 October, search <http://books.guardian.co.uk>.

3   Phil Day (2006) 'Bath Reading', in Findlay Lloyd (ed) (2006) *When Books Die*, Findlay Lloyd, Braidwood.

4   Tara Brabazon (2006) 'Directors Cut, July 2006', *Popular Culture Collective* <http://www.popularculturecollective.com/newsarchives/news0706.htm>.

5   Gary Frost (2005) 'Comments to Blogpost "Self-destructing books"', if: bookm a project of the institute of the future of the book <http://www.futureofthebook.org/blog/archives/2005/05/selfdestructing_books.html>.

6   A Jupiter Research study in February 2006 surveyed 3000 regular online users. It found that users spent 13 hours a week surfing the internet, which is equal to the time they spent watching TV. They spent one hour a week reading magazines, two hours reading newspapers and five hours listening to the radio. Thirty-seven per cent of people said they were reading fewer books as a result of their increased internet usage: Heidi Dawley (2006) 'Time-wise, Internet is now TV's Equal', *Media Life*, 1 February, search <http://www.medialifemagazine.com>.

7   John Updike, *New York Times* quoted in Nicholas Carr (2006) 'Keep your Edges Dry', *Roughtype*, 22 May, search <http://www.roughtype.com>.

8   Jane Austen (1996) *Pride and Prejudice*, Penguin Classics, London (first published 1813), p 3.

9   Of course, it's far more likely that I will download a mapping update for my in-car GPS navigation system, or get driving instructions from a mapping website than even own a street directory.

10 Alain de Botton (2006) 'Once Good, Twice Better', *Weekend Australian*, 25 March.

11 Bruce Sterling (1995) 'The Dead Media Project: A Modest Proposal and Public Appeal', Dead Media Project <http://www.deadmedia.org/modest-proposal.html>.

12 Dave Walsh (2001) 'Doing Sterling Work', *Irish Times*, 27 August. See <http://www.blather.net/articles/it_sterling_work.htm>.

13 At the time of writing, a pdf version of the book could be found via a BitTorrent search site such as isohunt.com.

14 Urban75 Editor (2004) 'Charing Corpse Road', *London Features*, February <http://www.urban75.org/london/charing.html>.

15 Associated Press (2006) 'Indie Bookstores Tackle Internet', *Wired*, 8 October, search <http://www.wired.com>.

16 Jason Epstein (2001) *Book Business*, WW Norton, New York, p 105.

17 David Kirkpatrick (2000) 'Report to the Authors Guild Midlist Books Study Committee', Authors Guild, pp 39–41 <http://www.authorsguild.org/miscfiles/midlist.pdf>.

18   ibid p 39.
19   Susan Wyndham (2006) 'Read, Read, Read, Chat, Chat, Chat', *Sydney Morning Herald* <http://blogs.smh.com.au/entertainment/archives/undercover/008294.html>.
20   Publib (2005) 'Library or Video Store? Does Anybody Read Anymore?' <http://lists.webjunction.org/wjlists/publib/2005-March/046167.html>.
21   'History of the British Library' <http://www.bl.uk/about/history.html>.
22   'Legal Deposit in the British Library' <http://www.bl.uk/about/policies/legaldeposit.html>.
23   Paula Berinstein (2006) 'How not to Run an Online Bookshop', *Writing Show* <http://writingshow.com/?page_id=87>.
24   See *World Book* <http://store.worldbook.com/wb/index.asp>.
25   For more discussion about book life cycles, see John B Thompson (2005) *Books in the Digital Age*, Polity Press, Cambridge, p 432.
26   'Unless you are Plato or Shakespeare, your book will disappear when there is no space left for it. Print is where words go to die.' Jeff Jarvis (2006) 'The Book is Dead, Long Live the Book', *Guardian*, 5 June <http://www.buzzmachine.com/index.php/books>.

▶▎   CHAPTER 7. Reconfigurations

1   Octave Uzanne (August 1894) 'The End of Books', *Scribner's 16*, p 224, quoted in Priscilla Murphy 'Books are Dead, Long live Books', in Henry Jenkins and David Thorburn (2003) *Rethinking Media Change*, MIT Press, Cambridge <http://web.mit.edu/transition/subs/murphy.html>.
2   Kevin Murray (1998) '(Sometimes) Brave New Australian Culture', *Art Monthly*, December 116, pp 14–15.
3   Voyager CD-ROM titles, 'The Institute for the Future of the Book' <http://www.futureofthebook.org>; Jeff Martin (2006) 'Voyager Company CD-ROMs, Production History and Preservation Challenges of Commercial Interactive Media, Electronic Arts Intermix' <http://resourceguide.eai.org/preservation/computer/pdf-docs/voyager_casestudy.pdf>.
4   Theodor H Nelson (1987) *Computer Lib/Dream Machines*, Microsoft Press, Seattle; Theodor H Nelson (1981) *Literary Machines*, Self-published, Swarthmore.
5   Vannevar Bush (July 1945) 'As We May Think', *Atlantic Monthly*, 176 <http://www.theatlantic.com/doc/194507/bush>.
6   Jakob Nielsen (1995) *Multimedia and Hypertext: The Internet and Beyond*, Morgan Kaufmann, San Francisco.
7   *Twelve Blue* <http://www.eastgate.com/TwelveBlue/Twelve_Blue.html>.
8   Jay David Bolter, 'Writing Space', *The Electronic Labyrinth* <http://elab.eserver.org/hfl0204.html>.
9   George Landow (1992) 'The Definition of Hypertext and Its History as a Concept', *Cyberarts and Cyberculture Initiative* <http://www.cyberartsweb.org/cpace/ht/jhup/history.html1>.
10   Christopher Keep, Tim McLaughlin, Robin Parmar (1993–2000) 'The End of the Book', *The Electronic Labyrinth* <http://elab.eserver.org/hfl0248.html>.
11   Kevin Kelly (2006) 'Scan this Book', *New York Times Magazine*, search

<http://www.nytimes.com>.

12   Paul Miller (2007) 'Google Planning on Getting into Books in a Big Way', *Engadget*, search <http://www.engadget.com>.

13   Brian Eno cited in Kevin Kelly (1995) 'Gossip is Philosophy', *Wired*, 3.05, May <http://www.wired.com/wired/archive/3.05/eno_pr.html>.

14   Interestingly, the institute was founded by Robert Stein, who started the Voyager Publishing Company mentioned previously.

15   Paula Berinstein (2006) 'What is a Networked Book?', *Writing Show*, 7 August, search <http://writingshow.com>.

16   Mackenzie Wark (2006) 'GAM3R 7H3ORY' <http://www.futureofthebook.org/gamertheory>.

17   Michael Duffy (2005) 'A Farewell to Publishing', *Sydney Morning Herald*, 15 October.

18   Tracy Mayor (2000) 'Book Industry Adapts to Digital Revolution', *CNN*, 20 September <http://edition.cnn.com/2000/TECH/computing/09/20/electrifying.book.industry.idg/index.html>.

19   Publishers reported 484 933 ebook units sold and $3 182 499 in revenue for the second quarter of 2005. They also reported 1024 ebooks published during this time. See Nick Bogaty (2006) 'Q2 2005 eBook Sales Statistics', *eBookit*, 21 March <http://www.ebookit.org/rubriche/news/ebook_sales_statistics.shtml>.

20   See Amanda Andrews (2006) 'Will Reader do For Books what iPod did for Music?', *Times*, 4 February, search <http://business.timesonline.co.uk>.

21   Quoted in David Carr (2005) 'Forget Blogs, Print Needs its own iPod', *New York Times*, 10 October, search <http://www.nytimes.com>.

22   'Camera buffs were stunned in January when Konica Minolta Holdings Inc, which traces its roots to 1873, said it was quitting the camera business altogether – digital and film – and selling its digital assets to rival Sony Corp. Nikon Corp said the same month it would stop making seven of its nine film cameras and concentrate on digital models. Fuji Photo Film Co, which plans to cut 5000 jobs, changed directions last month announcing it would spend nearly $8.5 million (US) to diversify into pharmaceuticals. Europe's biggest film maker, Germany's AgfaPhoto GmbH, couldn't adapt at all; it's now bankrupt and liquidated. Meanwhile, Antonio Perez, who is leading Eastman Kodak Co through a four-year digital remake, has warned that Kodak, the pioneer of point-and-shoot photography, is now "at the worst possible place" after a $1.03-billion third-quarter loss': quoted in Nate Anderson (2006) 'A Rough Decade for Traditional Camera Makers', *Arts Technica* <http://arstechnica.com/news.ars/post/20060418-6627.html>.

23   Burt Heim (2005) 'Curling up with a Good ebook', *BusinessWeek*, 29 December, search <http://www.businessweek.com>.

24   Some reviews for the Sony Reader can be found here: David Pogue (2006) 'Trying Again to Make Books Obsolete', *New York Times*, 12 October, search <http://www.nytimes.com>; Wade Roush (2006) 'A Good Read', *Technology Review*, MIT, 8 November, search <http://www.technologyreview.com>; Jim Milliot (2006) 'Sony Reader: Nice, but No iPod', *Publishers Weekly*, 2 October, search <http://www.publishersweekly.com>; Walter Mossberg (2006) 'Sony Reader Performs like a Good First Draft',

Wall Street Journal, 16 October, search <http://www.wsj.com>; Dan Costa (2006) 'Sony Portable Reader System (PRS-500)', *PCMag*, 18 October, search <http://www.pcmag.com>; Blake Wilson (2006) 'Has the iPod for Books Arrived?', *Slate*, 13 October, search <http://www.slate.com>; Alex Beam (2006) 'E-Books: Try to Read 'em and Weep', *Boston Globe*, 23 October, search <http://www.boston.com>.

▶▌   CHAPTER 8. The heavenly library

1   Known as Clarke's Third Law, found in Arthur C Clarke (1973) *Report on Planet Three and other Speculations,* Corgi, London.

2   A corollary of Clarke's Third Law, the origin of which seems to be disputed. Whilst widely attributed to Gregory Benford (see Rob Hyndman's blog <http://www.robhyndman.com/about-me/the-masthead-quote> and found in Gregory Benford (1997) *Foundation's Fear*, Orbit, London), it is perhaps originally the work of Dr Barry Gehm, and published in the science fiction magazine, *Analog* in 1991. Search for 'Clarke's Laws' at Professor Susan Stepney's factoids page at <http://www-users.cs.york.ac.uk/susan/cyc/l/law.htm>.

3   Nicholas Negroponte (1996) *Being Digital*, Hodder & Stoughton, London.

4   Charles Mann (2000) 'The Heavenly Jukebox', *Atlantic Monthly*, September 2000.

5   Mathew Honan (2007) 'iTunes Store Sales going Strong', *Playlist*, 9 January <http://playlistmag.com/news/2007/01/09/sales/index.php?lsrc=mwrss>.

6   Randall Chase (2006) 'Group Plans to Liquidate Tower Records', *ABC News*, 6 October, search <http://abcnews.go.com>.

7   '*The Australian*/Vogel Literary Award 2006 Judge's Report' <http://www.allenandunwin.com/Vogel/2006VogelReport.pdf>.

8   Gabriel Zaid (2003) *So Many Books*, Paul Dry Books, Philadelphia.

9   Michael Heyward quoted in Ramona Koval (2004) 'Books and Writing – The Fate of Fiction', *ABC Radio National*, 28 November <http://www.abc.net.au/rn/arts/bwriting/stories/s1252776.htm>.

10 Chris Anderson (2006) *The Long Tail*, Random House, London, p 76.

11 Jay David Bolter (2000) 'Writing Space', *Electronic Labyrinth* <http://elab.eserver.org/hfl0204.html>.

12 David Reay (2006) 'Publish and be Damned Wasteful', *Times Higher Education Supplement*, 13 October.

13 Nick Hampshire (2006) 'The Growing Environmental Case for E-books', *E-publishing Insights*, AFAICS Research Newsletter, 6 November <http://www.afaics.com>.

14 Jon Noring (2006) 'The IDPF Standards "Bandwagon"', *TeleRead* <http://www.teleread.org/blog/?p=5725>.

15 John B Thompson (2005) *Books in the Digital Age*, Polity, Cambridge, pp 412–420.

16 See Google Book Search Partner Program <https://books.google.com/partner>.

17 Jason Esptein (2006) 'Books@Google', *New York Review of Books*, 19 October <http://www.nybooks.com/articles/19436>.

18 Chris Anderson (2006) 'Universal's Long Tail Music Experiment', *The*

Long Tail Blog, 19 October <http://www.longtail.com>.

19   See Universal Music Enterprises UMe Portal <http://www.umeportal.com>.

20   Warner Press Relations (2005) 'Warner Music Group Launches Cordless Recordings', *Warner Music Group*, 10 November, go to <http://investors.wmg.com> click on 'News Releases' and '11/10/05'.

21   See Baen Free Library <http://www.baen.com/library>.

22   Moore's Law essentially argues that for the same cost, computer power doubles every 18 months; as demonstrated by the fact that my Casio wristwatch has more computing power than a military mainframe computer from three decades ago.

23   Alan Kay invented Smalltalk, and is considered a pioneer of the computer age. The full (1971) quote is: 'Don't worry about what anybody else is going to do … The best way to predict the future is to invent it. Really smart people with reasonable funding can do just about anything that doesn't violate too many of Newton's Laws!' <http://www.smalltalk.org/alankay.html>.

▶▶I Select bibliography

Anderson, Benedict (1991) *Imagined Communities*, Verso, London.
Anderson, Chris (2005) *The Long Tail*, Random House Business Books, London.
Berners-Lee, Tim (1999) *Weaving the Web*, Orion Business, London.
Birkerts, Sven (1994) *The Gutenberg Elegies*, Fawcett, Columbine.
Bragg, Melvyn (2006) *Twelve Books that Changed the World*, Hodder & Stoughton, London.
Carey, John (2005) *What Good are the Arts?*, Faber and Faber, London.
Cavallo, Guglielmo and Chartier, Roger (eds) (2003) *A History of Reading in the West*, Polity, Cambridge.
Cope, Bill and Philips, Angus (2006) *The Future of the Book in the Digital Age*, Chandos Publishing, Oxford.
Deleuze, Gilles and Guattari, Felix (1987) *A Thousand Plateaus* (B Massumi Trans), University of Minnesota Press, Minneapolis.
Eisenstein, Elizabeth (1997) *The Printing Press as an Agent of Change*, Cambridge University Press, Cambridge.
Epstein, Jason (2001) *Book Business*, WW Norton, New York.
Feldman, Gayle (2005) 'Best and Worst of Times: The Changing Business of Trade Books, 1975–2002', National Arts Journalism Program, Columbia University, New York.
Fischer, Steven Roger (2003) *A History of Reading*, Reaktion Books, London.
Gleick, James (1999) *Faster*, Abacus, London.
Graubard, Stephen (ed) (1983) *Reading in the 1980s*, RR Bowker, New York.
Habermas, Jürgen (1991) *The Structural Transformation of the Public Sphere*, MIT Press, Cambridge.
Hornby, Nick (2004) *The Polysyllabic Spree*, McSweeneys, San Francisco.
Jenkins, Henry (2006) *Convergence Culture – Where Old and New Media Collide*, New York University Press, New York.
Jones, Steve (ed) (1999) *Doing Internet Research*, Sage, Thousand Oaks.
Lanham, Richard A (1994) *The Electronic Word: Democracy, Technology and the Arts*, University of Chicago Press, London.
Levinson, Paul (1997) *The Soft Edge*, Routledge, London.
Lloyd, Findlay (ed) (2006) *When Books Die*, Findlay Lloyd, Braidwood.
Macleod, Jock and Buckridge, Pat (eds) (1992) *Books and Reading in Australian Society*, Institute for Cultural Policy Studies, Griffith University, Brisbane.
Manguel, Alberto (1996) *A History of Reading*, Penguin, London.
Marshall, David and Burnett, Robert (2003) *Web Theory*, Routledge, London.
McLuhan, Marshall (1962) *The Gutenberg Galaxy*, University of Toronto Press, Toronto.
Miller, Laura J (2006) *Reluctant Capitalists; Bookselling and the Culture of Consumption*, University of Chicago Press, Chicago.
Munro, Craig and Sheahan-Bright, Robyn (eds) (2006) *Paper Empires, A History*

of the Book in Australia 1946–2005, University of Queensland Press, Brisbane.

National Endowment for the Arts (2004) 'Reading at Risk: A Survey of Literary Reading in America', National Endowment for the Arts, Washington DC.

Negroponte, Nicholas (1996) *Being Digital*, Hodder & Stoughton, London.

Nielsen, Jakob (1995) *Multimedia and Hypertext: The Internet and Beyond*, Morgan Kaufmann, San Francisco.

Nunberg, Geoffrey (ed) (1996) *The Future of the Book*, University of California Press, Berkeley.

Ong, Walter (1988) *Orality & Literacy: The Technologizing of the Word*, Methuen, New York.

Postman, Neil (1986) *Amusing Ourselves to Death*, Penguin, New York.

Salwak, Dale (1999) *A Passion for Books*, Macmillan, London.

Schiffrin, André (2000) *The Business of Books*, Verso, London.

Sutherland, John (2006) *How to Read a Novel*, Profile Books, London.

Thompson, John B (1995) *Media and Modernity*, Polity Press, Cambridge.

— (2005) *Books in the Digital Age*, Polity Press, Cambridge.

Vise, David A (2005) *The Google Story*, Bantam Dell, New York.

Waters, Lindsay (2004) *Enemies of Promise, Publishing, Perishing and The Eclipse of Scholarship*, Prickly Paradigm Press, Chicago.

Watts, Ian (2000) *The Rise of the Novel: Studies in Defoe, Richardson and Fielding*, Pimlico, London.

Zaid, Gabriel (2003) *So Many Books*, Paul Dry Books, Philadelphia.

▶▶▎ Index